The Fragile X Syndrome

Edited by

KAY E. DAVIES

Institute for Molecular Medicine
John Radcliffe Hospital
Oxford

Oxford New York Tokyo

OXFORD UNIVERSITY PRESS

1989

Oxford University Press, Walton Street, Oxford OX2 6DP
Oxford New York Toronto
Delhi Bombay Calcutta Madras Karachi
Petaling Jaya Singapore Hong Kong Tokyo
Nairobi Dar es Salaam Cape Town
Melbourne Auckland
and associated companies in
Berlin Ibadan

Oxford is a trade mark of Oxford University Press

British Library Cataloguing in Publication Data
The fragile X syndrome
1. Man. Mental retardation
I. Davies, K. E. (Kay E.) II. Series
616.85′88
ISBN 0–19–261836–9

Library of Congress Cataloging in Publication Data
The fragile X syndrome
(Molecular medicine)
Includes bibliographies.
1. Fragile X syndrome. I. Davies, Kay. II. Series:
Molecular medicine (Oxford, England) [DNLM: 1. Chromosome Abnormalities—genetics. 2. Linkage (Genetics).
3. Mental Retardation—genetics. QS 677 X112]
RJ506.F73X16 1989 616.85′88042 88-33025
ISBN 0–19–261836–9 (pbk.)

Typeset by Cotswold Typesetting Ltd, Cheltenham

Printed in Great Britain
at Butler & Tanner Ltd, Frome, Somerset

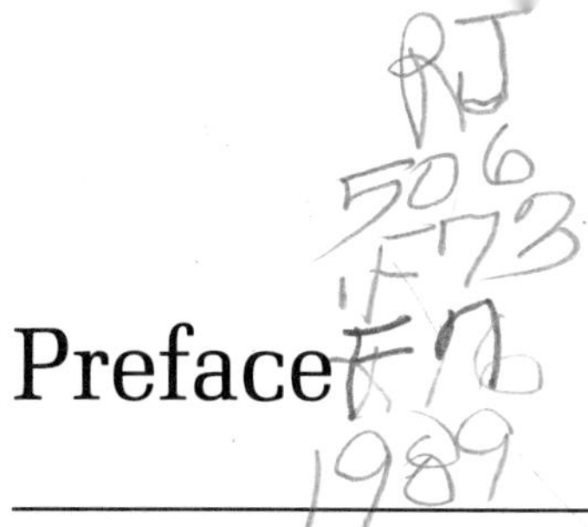

Preface

The fragile X syndrome is currently attracting much interest because it is now recognized as the most common genetic cause of mental retardation after Down's syndrome. No effective treatment is yet available and the underlying biochemical defect is not understood. Diagnosis can be made on the basis of the appearance of a gap in the X chromosome when lymphocytes are cultured under certain conditions. Genetic counselling is often difficult because although it primarily affects males, one third of carrier females are also retarded. In addition, about one fifth of males that inherit the mutation appear phenotypically normal. These observations have prompted extensive clinical, epidemiological, and cytogenetic studies of the fragile X syndrome. The important observations are reviewed in this volume.

In the absence of an effective treatment, this disorder is a major challenge for molecular medicine. As the fourth chapter in the book indicates, identification of the gene, or genes, involved should explain the fascinating inheritance pattern and be the first step in designing rational treatments in the future. Furthermore, these studies are leading to more extensive analyses of other forms of X-linked mental retardation not associated with any cytogenetic marker.

MRC External Staff
Institute of Molecular Medicine,
Oxford
November 1988

K. E. D.

Contents

Contributors

W. Ted Brown, *Chairman, Department of Human Genetics, NYS Institute for Basic Research in Developmental Disabilities, 1050 Forest Hill Road, Staten Island, New York 10314, USA.*

Jean-Pierre Fryns, *Division of Human Genetics, University Hospital Gasthuisberg, Saint-Rafael Gasthuisberg, Herestraat 49, B-3000 Leuven, Belgium.*

Randi Hagerman, *Department of Pediatrics, University of Colorado Health Sciences Center, Child Development Unit, Children's Hospital, 1056 East 19th Avenue, Denver, Colorado 80220, USA*

Niels Tommerup, *Department of Medical Genetics, The John F. Kennedy Institute, DK-2600 Glostrup, Denmark.*

Tessa Webb, *Department of Clinical Genetics, Birmingham Maternity Hospital, Queen Elizabeth Maternity Hospital, Birmingham B15 2TG, UK.*

1 X-linked mental retardation and the fragile X syndrome: a clinical approach

JEAN-PIERRE FRYNS

Introduction

After the discovery of the fragile X syndrome, the field of X-linked mental retardation has exploded over the past 10 years. The importance of early diagnosis of this most frequent cause of mental retardation has now overall been recognized. A better knowledge of the clinical, and even of the more fundamental, aspects of this condition is not only important for clinical geneticists but for all medical professions and, in fact, for all who are interested in and/or have to care for the mentally retarded.

Historical perspectives

In industrialized countries, about 2–3 per cent of the general population are believed to be mentally retarded (Priest *et al.* 1961; Bundey and Carter 1974). The aetiology of this mental handicap is heterogeneous, and, up to a few years ago, for a large group of these mentally disabled no aetiology was known.

In 1938 L. S. Penrose published: *A clinical and genetic study of 1280 cases of mental retardation* from the Royal Eastern Counties Institution, Colchester, England. In the preface, it is stated 'there can be no doubt that Dr. Penrose's methods, data and results will to a large extent determine the general course of research in mental deficiency in this country for some years to come.'

A major increase in the medical interest in the mentally retarded has been noted since the early sixties, and was mainly stimulated by a better progressive understanding of biological mechanisms involved in the causation of mental retardation. Several factors have stimulated this increased interest in research in mental retardation.

1. The discovery that a chromosomal anomaly, trisomy 21, was the cause of Down syndrome led to the description of other syndromes related to specific chromosomal abnormalities (de Grouchy and Turleau 1977). Except for a small number of sex-chromosome anomalies, these other entities were mostly discovered during studies of the mentally retarded. With the introduction of different chromosome-banding techniques in 1970, the number of constitutional chromosomal syndromes increased to more than 120. More recently, prometaphase chromosome studies have revealed small chromosomal alterations in a number of previously delineated clinical syndromes, e.g. Prader–Willi syndrome (Hawkey and Smithies 1976) and tricho-rhino-phalangeal syndrome (Fryns and Van den Berghe 1986).

2. In the same period, genetic counselling services were progressively established in university hospitals of industrialized countries. Individuals, couples, and families confronted with the occurrence of mental retardation have, from the beginning, been the largest and the most difficult group attending counselling clinics. Further research in the aetiology of mental retardation therefore became necessary, as the quality of genetic counselling is directly dependent on the accuracy of aetiological diagnosis.

3. An increased number of mental retardation–multiple malformation syndromes is currently being delineated by careful clinical observations of malformed stillborn neonates and of children and adults with malformative stigmata (Smith 1982).

4. Up to now, the discovery of X-linked mental retardation with or without Xq27.3 fragility was the last but most important step in the development of great interest in the biology of mental retardation. The considerable excess of male mental retardates had been noted for several decades (Johnson 1897; Goddard 1914; Priest *et al.* 1961; Reed and Reed 1965). Moreover, in the same period an increasing number of individual families were reported in whom 'non-specific mental retardation' was inherited in a pattern consistent with X-linkage. Table 1.1 gives a review of the reported families in the pre-fragile X period. At that time an impressive and steadily increasing number of conditions were also individualized in which mental retardation was one of the features of an otherwise clinically recognizable multiple malformation syndrome. Table 1.2 summarizes these X-linked syndromes reported up to 1976. A remarkable contribution to the delineation of X-linked mental retardation was made by Lehrke (1972, 1974) in the late sixties to early seventies. In his thesis *X-linked mental retardation and verbal disability* he was the first to note that the most specific feature of males with

Table 1.1. Individual family studies from the literature

Author	Number of families	Number of boys	IQ	Speech development
Martin and Bell 1943	1	11	very low	very poor
Allan *et al.* 1944	1	22		poor
Dunn *et al.* 1963	1	20	poor	
Renpenning *et al.* 1963	1	21	15–45	poor
Opitz *et al.* 1965	1	20	from very low to 60	
Neuhäuser *et al.* 1969	3	17	low	disturbed
Snyder and Robinson 1969	1	9		poor
Lubs 1969	1	4	mild to severe	
Turner and Turner 1974	5	25	36–51	
Schönenberg and Böttcher 1974	1	5	idiocy and imbecility	poor
Lehrke 1974	5	52	from very low to 85	very poor
Steel and Chorazy 1974	1	6	low	
Yarborough and Howard-Peebles 1976	1	19		very poor

X-linked mental retardation was verbal dysfunctioning, with higher scores on performance than on verbal IQ testing.

It was, however, only after the description of the fragile Xq27 site by Lubs in 1969, and the report of the association of this fragile X site, and its folic-acid-dependent expression, with mental retardation (Sutherland 1977) that the existence of X-linked mental retardation was fully accepted. In the period 1977–82 the interest in X-linked mental retardation has been primarily focused on the fragile X syndrome (Sutherland 1979; Herbst 1980; Herbst and Miller 1980; Jacobs *et al.* 1980; Turner and Opitz 1980; Turner *et al.* 1980; Mattei *et al.* 1981; Carpenter *et al.* 1982; Blomquist *et al.* 1983; Fryns 1984; Opitz and Sutherland 1984; Sherman *et al.* 1984). Since 1983 three international workshops on the fragile X syndrome and X-linked mental retardation have been organized, covering all fascinating aspects of these conditions. Of the families reported before the fragile X screening, some have turned out to be fragile X positive (e.g. the family reported by Martin and Bell 1943) while others are fragile X negative (e.g. the Renpenning families: Renpenning *et al.* 1963).

Further experience in the fragile X syndrome has shown that 'the non-specific mental retardation' syndrome in fragile X positive adult males is associated, in two-thirds of them, with a clinically recognizable triad: moderate mental retardation; large, long face with long, everted ears; and megalotestes. These features were already present in the mentally retarded males of the family reported by Martin and Bell (1943) and,

Table 1.2. X-linked syndromes that may involve mental retardation in some or all cases (adapted from McKusick 1986)

Addison's disease and cerebral sclerosis
Allbright hereditary osteodystrophy
Börjeson syndrome
Bullous dystrophy, hereditary macular type
Congenital total cataract
Pelizaeus Merzbacher disease
Partial agenesis of corpus callosum
Cutis verticis gyrata, thryoid aplasia, and M.R.
Nephrogenic diabetes insipidus
Neurohypophyseal type of diabetes insipidus
Anhidrotic ectodermal dysplasia
Hydrocephalus due to congenital stenosis of aqueduct of Sylvius
Hyperparathyroidism
Lesh–Nyhan syndrome
Microphtalmia
Mucopolysaccharidosis type II
Pseudohypertrophic muscular dystrophy
Norrie disease—atrophia bulborum hereditaria
Optic atrophy—spastic paraplegia syndrome
Pain syndrome
Pseudoglioma
Van den Bosch syndrome
Mental retardation with bilateral enlargement of the testes without any endocrinological disturbance (Turner *et al.* 1975).
Mental retardation with overdevelopment of the genitalia (Escalanté *et al.* 1971)
Mental retardation with megalocephaly and myopia (Walker 1973)
with imperforate anus, vertebral anomalies, and congenital heart disease (Walker 1973)
with hyperactivity and apparent defect in the methylation of sympathetic amines (Walker 1973)
Mental retardation and/or hydrocephalus (Fried 1972)
Coffin syndrome (Coffin *et al.* 1966)
X-linked skeletal dysplasia with mental retardation (Christian *et al.* 1977)

therefore, this characteristic adult phenotype is called the 'Martin–Bell phenotype'.

Present data on X-linked mental retardation (*Proceedings of the Third International Workshop on the Fragile X and X-linked Mental Retardation* 1988) confirm that fragile X screening is positive in no more than 40–50 per cent of the males with X-linked mental retardation. In the group of so-called non-specific mental retardation, an increasing number of new, clinically distinct entities have been delineated: considering the X-linked syndromes in which mental retardation can be associated, a total of 69 different entities have been reported up to now (McKusick 1986).

The fragile X syndrome

The fragile X syndrome has generally been recognized as one of the major causes of mental retardation in all populations and ethnic groups

(Venter *et al.* 1986). Next to trisomy 21, the fragile X syndrome is the most common specific cause of mental retardation among mentally retarded boys. Recent epidemiological studies indicate that the incidence of the syndrome in children of school age is 1 in 1.360–1.500 for boys and 1 in 2.073 for girls.

A better knowledge of the clinical characteristics of this syndrome is very important, not only for clinical geneticists, but also for other medical professions, psychologists, social nurses, and for all workers interested in the field of mental retardation. Recognition of the clinical features may lead to early diagnosis, a *sine qua non* for better help of the disabled, and for information and genetic counselling for families and relatives.

The postpubertal fragile X males

General description of the phenotype

In postpubertal males, the fragile X syndrome may be associated with a characteristic clinical triad: moderate mental retardation, long face with large everted ears, and macro-orchidism, i.e. the so-called Martin–Bell phenotype (Sutherland and Ashforth 1979; Herbst 1980; Jacobs *et al.* 1980; Jennings *et al.* 1980; Turner *et al.* 1980; Herbst *et al.* 1981; Mattei *et al.* 1981; Carpenter 1983; Engel 1983; Jacobs *et al.* 1983; Fryns 1984; Meryash *et al.* 1984; Opitz and Sutherland 1984). In the clinically typical fragile X positive male the face is long with large, everted ears and mandibular prognathism; the forehead is large and quadrangular with relative macrocephaly (Fig. 1.1a–d). Facial features are coarsened because of slight oedema and thickening of the subcutaneous tissue. In addition to macro-orchidism, general macrogenitosomia with hyper-pigmentation of the scrotum occurs in at least half of the patients. Systematic fragile screening studies of mentally retarded male populations have demonstrated, however, that the typical triad is present in only 60 per cent of fragile X positive adult males (Jacobs *et al.* 1980; Herbst *et al.* 1981; Mattei *et al.* 1981) (Fig. 1.2a, b).

In 10 per cent of the fragile X positive males with typical faces and macro-orchidism, the mental retardation is deep; and about the same percentage of males combine moderate mental retardation and macro-testes without a typical face. Macro-orchidism is absent in 25–30 per cent of all fragile X positive adult males. In at least 10 per cent of affected males mental retardation is the only presenting symptom, and the diagnosis of fragile X could easily be missed if the clinical selection criterion for fragile X study were only to be the presence of megalo-testes. Moreover, as will be further discussed in this chapter, megalo-testes occur in the mentally retarded in a number of conditions not related to the fragile X syndrome.

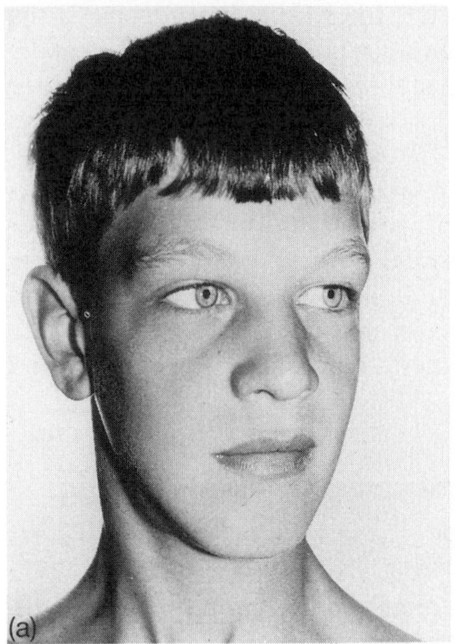

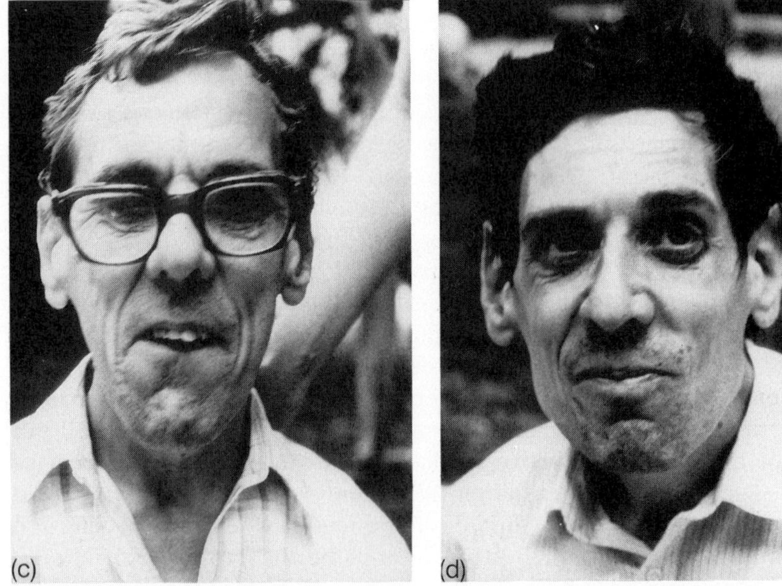

Fig. 1.1. Adult fragile X positive males with typical facial featurs.

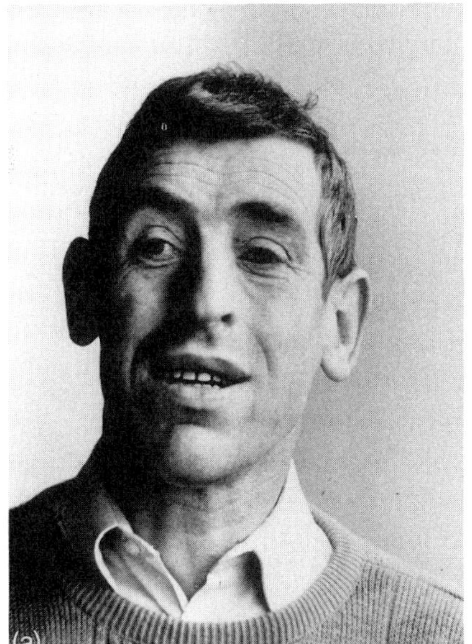

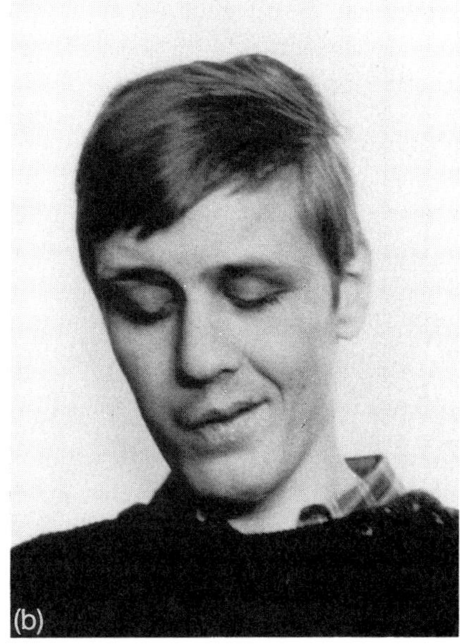

Fig. 1.2. Two adult fragile X positive males of nearly normal appearance.

A great intrafamilial variability of the phenotype has been observed in different pedigrees (Fryns *et al.* 1984*b*). Up to now, no clearcut correlation could be found between mental status, phenotype, and fragile X expression. Moreover, a large intrafamilial variability may also exist for these parameters. Analysis of fragile X expression with age shows a small but significant drop after the age of 40 (Turner and Partington 1987).

A connective tissue dysplasia in the fragile X syndrome?

Several clinical features of the fragile X syndrome, including hyperextensible joints, large ears, mitral valve prolapse, and aortic root dilatation, have been evocated by several authors as suggestive of a connective tissue dysplasia (Loehr *et al.* 1986; Waldstein *et al.* 1987). The first group of authors found mitral valve prolapse in 80 per cent of fragile X males older than 18 years, and 'mild aortic root dilatation' in 7 of the 34 males examined. Waldstein *et al.* (1987) reported on an 18-year-old male with fragile X syndrome and severe tubular hypoplasia of the descending aorta, with mild coarctation, cardiomegaly, and left ventricular hypertrophy. Microscopy revealed thickened, irregular, and blurred elastin fibres in the valve insertions and the arteries. Up to now, no distinct biochemical abnormalities have been documented in the fragile X syndrome as a possible explanation of these distinct anatomical changes observed in a few patients. Although these observations may be important, they do not correlate with the available data on survival in the fragile X syndrome. There are no reports of sudden cardiovascular collapse in fragile X patients, nor is long-term life expectancy compromised (Fryns 1984). Of all mentally disabled, the fragile X syndrome has by far the best life prognosis, which does not seem to differ greatly from that of a normal population.

The nature and origin of macro-orchidism in fragile X males has been a matter of discussion in the past. Some authors have interpreted the large testes as another indication of connective tissue dysplasia (Loehr *et al.* 1986; Waldstein *et al.* 1987). They reported increased testicular interstitium and patulous seminiferous tubules. Others (Fryns *et al.* 1988*c*) could not confirm the presence of specific histological abnormalities in these large testes, which may be present from birth.

The concurrence of Klinefelter syndrome and fragile X syndrome

Considering the frequency of Klinefelter syndrome and the fragile X syndrome, the simultaneous occurrence of both conditions in the same patient could be expected occasionally. During the past few years several patients with this association have been reported (Jacobs *et al.* 1980; Wilmot *et al.* 1980; Froster-Iskenius *et al.* 1982; Froster-Iskenius *et al.* 1983). In the Leuven fragile X screening programme three Klinefelter patients were found to be fragile X positive. Up to now, 142 fragile X positive, apparently unrelated index patients were diagnosed in this study, bringing the total number of fragile X positive males in our centre to 465. In our studies we found one in 155 fragile X positive male patients to have, in addition, a 47,XXY chromosome abnormality. In the first patient (Fryns *et al.* 1983), we found both conditions associated in a slightly to moderately mentally retarded male with XY/XXY mosaicism and fragile X. The fragile X was heterozygously expressed only on the XXY cell-line and, except for the mental retardation, this male presented a typical Klinefelter phenotype, with gynecoid habitus and small, soft testes. He had a round, normal face in comparison to the long face with large everted ears in his marker X brother who had 46 chromosomes and severe mental retardation. In the second 47,XXY patient with a typical fragile X syndrome phenotype (Fryns *et al.* 1984*c*), we found homozygous fragile X expression. This patient presented a typical long face with mandibular prognathism, but the gonadal development was still consistent with the classical findings of Klinefelter syndrome. The third patient (Fig. 1.3a, b) is slightly mentally retarded, but, in addition to the general Klinefelter habitus and hypogonadism, he has also the typical long fragile X face. Fragile X screening was positive in 4 per cent of the cells, showing Xq27 fragility of one of both X-chromosomes.

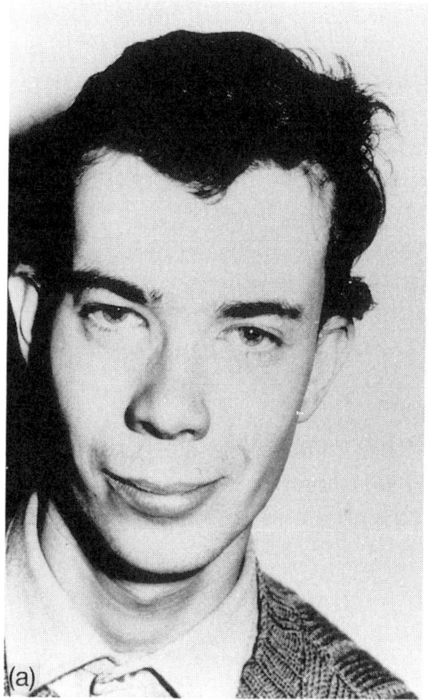

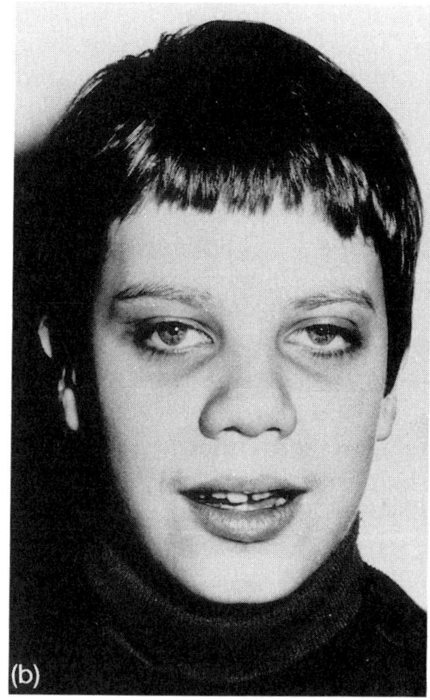

Fig. 1.3. The fragile X positive Klinefelter patient (a) and his fragile X positive brother (b).

The present data on patients with the Klinefelter syndrome/fragile X association confirm that, except for the mental retardation and the long face, their phenotype is much more influenced by the 47,XXY chromosome constitution than by the presence of a fragile X syndrome. The genital development in all patients is consistent with the classical findings in Klinefelter syndrome patients.

The finding of a 47,XXY chromosome constitution in three out of 465 fragile X positive males, as mentioned above, is much higher than we could have expected by chance. At the present time, scant data exist on the possible association of non-disjunction and the marker X. Brøndum-Nielsen *et al.* (1983*b*) found in her cytogenetic study of 23 obligate and 45 potential carriers 11.4 per cent X-aneuploid cells in the obligate carriers compared to only 1.3 per cent aneuploid cells in potential carriers. The difference was independent from the known age-related loss of X-chromosomes in older women. In young obligate carriers she found 9 per cent X-aneuploidies, mainly triple-X, while only 1.2 per cent X-aneuploidies were observed in the potential carrier group. In his study on the origin of the extra 21 chromosome, Tommerup (see pp. 45–6 in

Turner *et al.* 1986) identified fragile site in one of the parents of five out of 223 trisomy 21 cases.

Although the present data need further confirmation, they suggest an increased tendency to non-disjunction in female fragile X carriers.

A peculiar subphenotype in the fragile X syndrome? Extreme obesity, short stature, stubby hands and feet, diffuse hyperpigmentation (Fig. 1.4a and b)

As discussed above, the 'classical phenotype' of fragile X positive males is that of a moderately mentally retarded male with large testes and typical, long face. During the past years we have been impressed by a peculiar subphenotype which we observed in at least eight fragile X positive males: macrocephaly, short stature, acromegaloid features with facial plethora, short, broad hands and feet, and stubby fingers and toes (Fig. 1.4a, b). Adult males presented a characteristic periorbital hyper-pigmentation, and the same pigmentation anomaly was seen in the

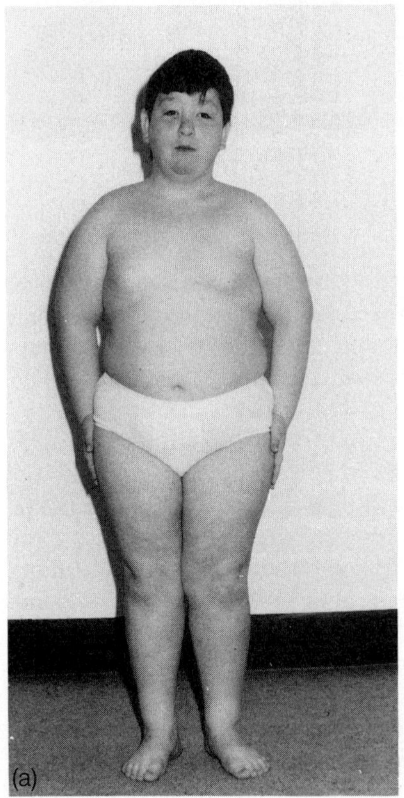

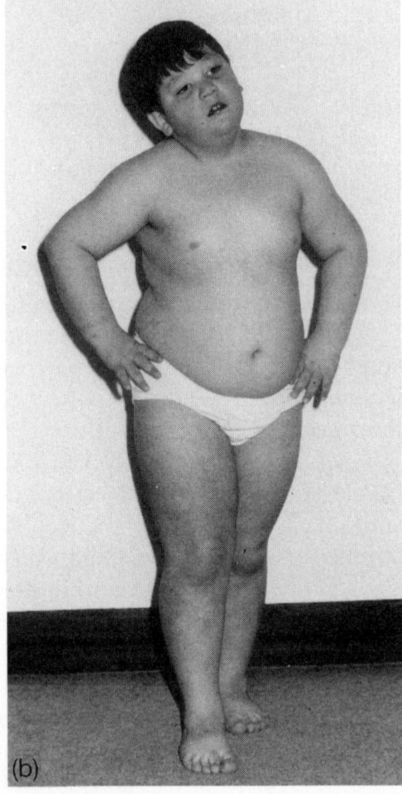

Fig. 1.4. The peculiar Prader–Willi-like phenotype in two brothers.

axillary and genital regions. The findings of this Prader–Willi-like phenotype in an increasing number of fragile X males may be another indication for a disturbed function of the cortico-hypothalamo-hypophyseal axis in this syndrome (Fryns *et al.* 1988*b*) as will be further discussed.

Phenocopies of the fragile X syndrome: partial fragile X phenotype with megalotestes in fragile X negative patients with acquired lesions of the central nervous system

In all fragile X screening programmes of institutionalized male retardates, a variable number of fragile X negative macro-orchidic males is detected. Some of these patients present a specific fragile X negative type of X-linked mental retardation. In others, anamnestic data and detailed CNS examinations are in favour of acquired CNS lesions as the cause of their phenotypic abnormalities and macro-orchidism. Recently we reported three men with acquired lesions of the CNS (one male with tumour of the third ventricle, two males with peri- and postnatal accidents). In all three patients macro-orchidism was associated with facial features similar to those found in fragile X males, but they were fragile X negative. The finding of megalotestes associated with a partial fragile X phenotype in the present patients and, more particularly, the documentation of a hypothalamic tumour in one patient, suggests that a specific hypothalamic lesion in fragile X males is responsible for some of their manifestations.

The Martin–Bell phenotype without fragile X: does it exist?

During the past there has been much discussion as to whether the Martin–Bell phenotype really exists without fragile X expression. At the present time there seems to be insufficient evidence to answer this question. As discussed above, a Martin–Bell-like phenotype with macrocephaly, long face, and large testes may occur in patients with acquired CNS lesions. Secondly, several fragile X positive families have been documented over the past years in which one or more 'Martin–Bell males' present a negative fragile X screening, or have an extremely low percentage of fragile X positive cells even after repeated screenings in different lymphocyte cultures with different culture conditions. Figure 1.5 gives a clear illustration of this type of situation: fragile X screening in the first of the three mentally retarded brothers with typical Martin–Bell phenotype remained negative despite all possible cytogenetic efforts. Up to now, and as far as we know, however, no family has been reported with a typical Martin–Bell phenotype in the mentally retarded males, and in which fragile X screening is negative in all retarded male patients.

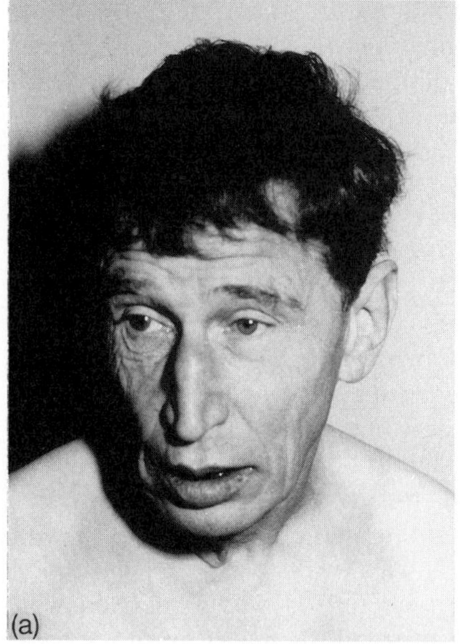

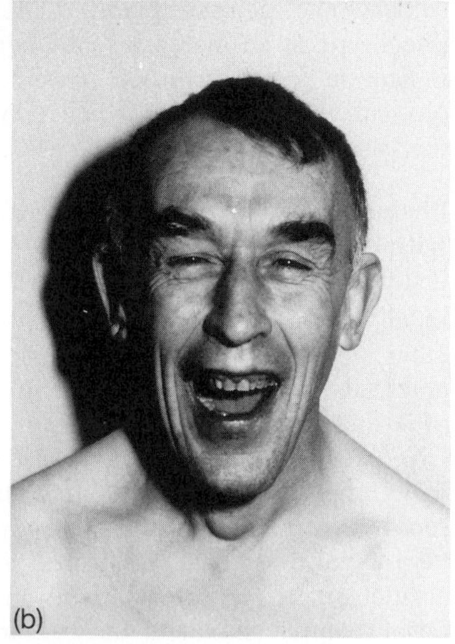

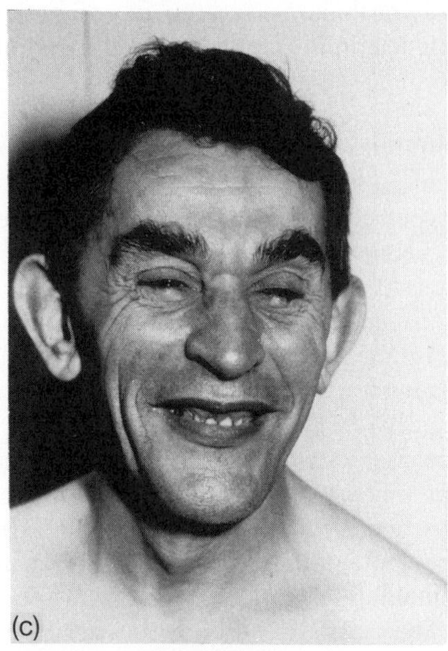

Fig. 1.5. Three brothers (a, b, c) with typical Martin–Bell phenotype. Fragile X screening remained negative in one of them (a) on three different occasions.

Thus far, the available data indicate that the Martin–Bell phenotype associated with X-linked mental retardation can occur without fragile X expression, but this seems to be less frequent than the concurrence of X-linked mental retardation and positive fragile X expression without the Martin–Bell phenotype.

The 'normal' male transmitter

Male transmission of the fragile X syndrome has been well documented. In the original family described by Martin and Bell (1943) two unaffected brothers had passed on the gene for the fragile X syndrome through their healthy daughters to the next generations in which 11 mentally retarded males were observed. The phenomenon of non-manifesting carriers transmitting the gene for X-linked mental retardation and fragile X has since then been repeatedly observed, and is an apparently frequent condition (Webb *et al.* 1981; Fryns and Van den Berghe 1982; Froster-Iskenius *et al.* 1986). In 140 families studied in Leuven, evidence for transmission of the fragile X chromosome through normal male(s) was present in at least 15 cases. Figure 1.6 illustrates such a pedigree. Fragile X syndrome was found in two boys (IV, 6 and IV, 10); their mothers were sisters (III, 4 and III, 7) and further examination of the family confirmed the diagnosis of fragile X syndrome in two of their paternal nephews (III, 9 and III, 14) and one paternal niece (III, 13). How puzzling pedigree findings in the fragile X syndrome

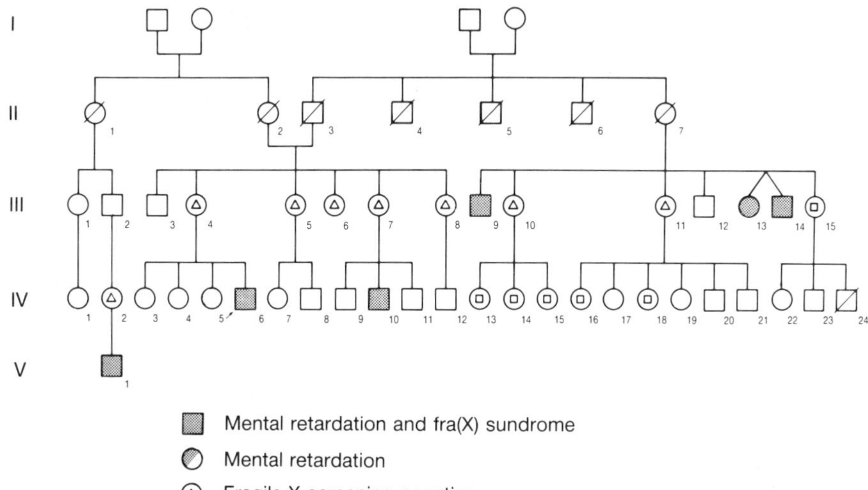

Fig. 1.6. Pedigree 1.

may be is further illustrated by the finding, one year later, of a definite case of the syndrome in a boy (V, 1) in the maternal side of the family. In a number of other families (Fig. 1.7), the occurrence of fragile X syndrome in several maternal nephews (Fig. 1.8), together with true macrocephaly in the maternal grandfather (Fig. 1.9) with negative fragile X screening, may also be an indication of probable male transmission. In these types of pedigrees the normal transmitting males do not show the marker (negative fragile X screening), but transmit the trait to their daughters.

Available studies do not allow a precise estimate of the ratio of mentally normal versus subnormal males with positive fragile X. Based

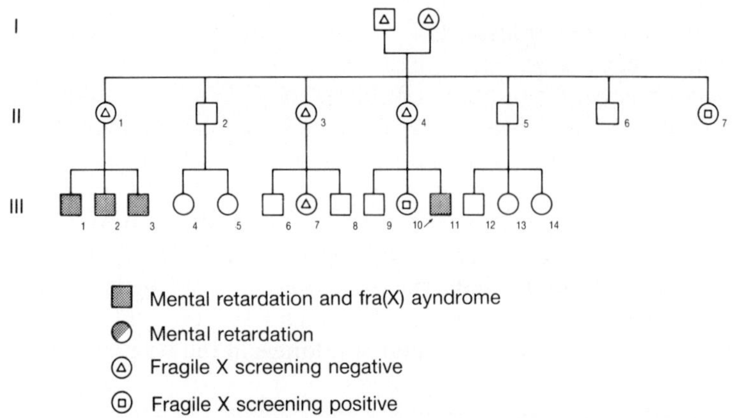

Fig. 1.7. Pedigree 2.

Fig. 1.8. Three fragile X positive boys (III, 1; III, 2; III, 11—pedigree 2) with variable facial features.

Fig. 1.9. The maternal grandfather (I, 1—pedigree 2) with macrocephaly and relatively long face.

upon data in prepubertal boys, at least 10–15 per cent of fragile X expressing males may have a sufficiently high level of mental performance to make reproduction socially possible and acceptable.

The prepubertal phenotype in the fragile X syndrome

General data

In prepubertal males, clinical signs are much more non-specific (Fig. 1.10a, b) and in only 40–50 per cent of young fragile X males is moderate mental retardation associated with facial abnormalities, of which relative macrocephaly is more striking than long face and large everted ears. Macrogenitosomia is a relatively rare finding (5–10 per cent) in the prepubertal males. It has become evident that the phenotype of the fragile X syndrome includes a whole scale of physical disturbances, including disturbed growth and development (Fryns 1984). In their early years, most boys present clinically with an overgrowth syndrome with macrocephaly, large fontanelle, and body measurements exceeding the 97 percentile. In that period differential diagnosis from cerebral gigantism is nearly impossible on clinical grounds only (Beemer *et al.* 1986; Fryns 1984) (Fig. 1.11a, b). From the available experience it has become clear that in all patients, males and females, in whom the diagnosis of Sotos syndrome has been previously made, a fragile X screening should be performed. It appears now that cerebral gigantism is

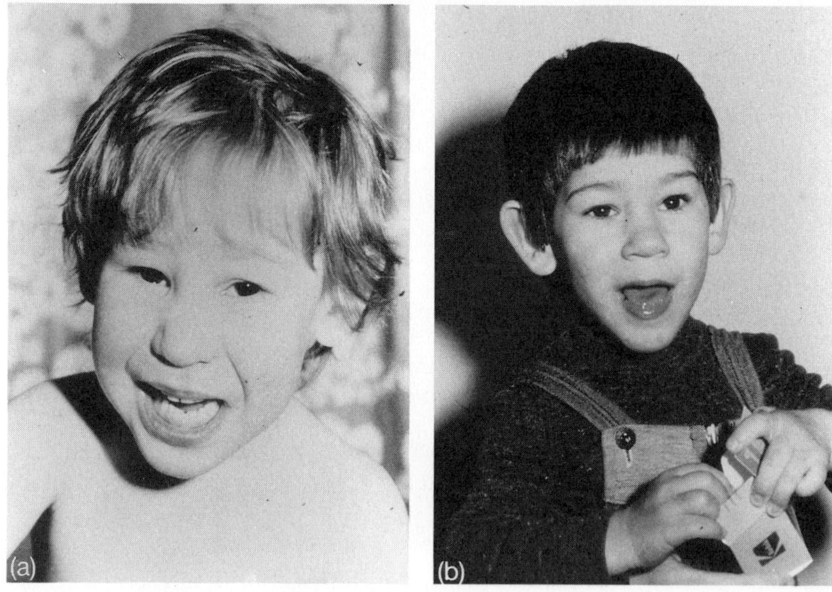

Fig. 1.10. The facial oedema in young fragile X boys.

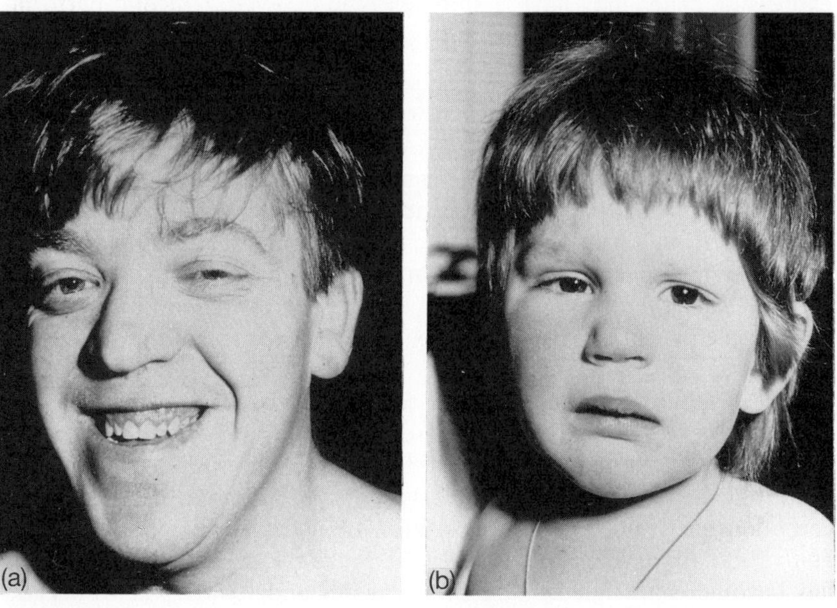

Fig. 1.11. The overgrowth syndrome with evident macrocephaly in a 24-year-old fragile X positive male and his 2.5-year-old maternal nephew.

rather a sequence than a syndrome. The clinical overgrowth syndrome in the fragile X patients is apparently related with a CNS disturbance, probably in the hypothalamic region, as males with acquired CNS lesions in that region present a fragile X-like phenotype (see above).

More characteristic, however, is the apparently typical psychological profile in young fragile X boys: regardless of the IQ level, they present with severe hyperkinetic behaviour, emotional instability, hypersensitivity, handbiting, and autistic features. In Leuven, an ongoing evaluation of the psychological profiles in young fragile X boys and boys with so-called idiopathic developmental retardation shows relevant quantitative differences. Fragile X pre-school boys present, in general, mild to moderate mental retardation with severe delay in speech development. Impulsive, hyperactive behaviour problems are more frequent and more intense than in control groups. Autistic features are most pronounced in the group of fragile X boys with IQ below 55 (Fryns 1984; Borghgraef *et al.* 1987). These symptoms progressively disappear after puberty and, at least in our experience, they were not influenced by folic acid treatment.

Neurological symptoms, epilepsy, and Sudden Infant Death (SID)

It is now well established that in an important number (± 30 per cent) of fragile X males anamnestic data reveal pre-, peri-, or postnatal complications, e.g. prematurity, perinatal asphyxia, neonatal convulsions, or epilepsy. Careful neurological examination reveals in some fragile X boys additional abnormalities such as generalized hyper-reflexia, spastic paraplegia, and strabismus. It is therefore not surprising to note that before fragile X screening the origin of mental handicap of at least 20 per cent of the fragile X patients diagnosed was thought to be of acquired origin (Fryns 1984). Musumeci *et al.* (1987) reported typical temporal spike activities on sleep EEG in more than 50 per cent of the fragile X males. The precise aetiology of these neurological symptoms is unknown at the present time, but may be related to a period of transient, increased intracerebral pressure, as suggested by the finding of mild ventricular dilatation on computer tomographic scanning of fragile X boys younger than 1 year (Fryns 1984). On the other hand, extensive macro- and microscopic examination of the CNS in two other young boys did not disclose an anatomic abnormality (Fryns *et al.* 1988*c*). Another puzzling finding which may be related to the increased tendency to CNS complications in the fragile X syndrome is the apparently significant increase of sudden death (SID) in fragile X children (Fryns *et al.* 1988*c*). In eight fragile X positive families with so-called non-specific familial mental retardation and a mentally subnormal mother, 68 children were born. Two boys and four girls (i.e. 6/68 liveborn children) died unexpectedly before the age of 1 year. We observed also a high, unexplained mortality in the progeny of 86 mentally normal, obligate carrier females: 17 deaths before the age of 18 months out of a total of 219 male offspring, and six deaths out of a total of 169 female offspring. Confirmation of these data is urgently needed by a world-wide, prospective, and appropriate controlled study of this phenomenon, and may stimulate further research towards the fundamental CNS disturbances both in the SID and the fragile X syndromes.

The female and the fragile X

General data

One of the most difficult problems in the fragile X or Martin–Bell syndrome is that of the female carriers. The investigations on female carriers were not only concerned with the cytogenetic difficulties related to the fragile X expression in the female, but increasingly uncovered the consequences for the mental status and the phenotype of female fragile X carriers (Fryns 1986; Kemper *et al.* 1986; Partington 1986). In our study of 144 female heterozygotes, 46 had subnormal intelligence. An IQ between 85 and 70 was present in 26 cases and most of these had more or less serious problems in the management of their family tasks and with difficulties in raising their children. For five of them regular psychiatric admissions were necessary because of chronic psychotic problems. The IQ was between 70 and 55 in 11 carriers; nine others were markedly mentally retarded.

Partial clinical manifestiations in the carriers were common (28 per cent), and facial features included a high, broad forehead, long face, and mandibular prognathism. Partial phenotypic expression was more common in the mentally subnormal females (55 per cent), but was not rare in the mentally normal carriers (14 per cent) (Fig. 1.12).

Fragile X testing in carriers is disappointing. In the normal female heterozygote repeated tests for the fragile X remain negative in more than 50 per cent of cases. The limitations of the cytogenetic techniques in fragile X carrier detection create great difficulties for accurate genetic counselling of the individual female at risk. Whereas fragile X expression is influenced somewhat by age and mental level of the carrier, the most important factor is the phenotype. In all females with partial phenotypic expression, the fragile X was present regardless of age and mental level. Careful clinical examination of female relatives of fragile X males provides valuable and definite information with regard to the carrier status in individual women.

Inactivation pattern of the fragile X in heterozygous carriers

The reasons why some heterozygous females are mentally handicapped

Fig. 1.12. Typical 'fragile X facial stigmata' in female heterozygotes.

while others have normal intelligence, and why they express such different phenotypic changes still remain obscure. One possible explanation is a difference due to activation or inactivation of the fragile X. Different groups (Jacobs *et al.* 1980; Uchida and Joyce 1982; Brøndum-Nielsen *et al.* 1983*b*; Fryns *et al.* 1984*a*; Knoll *et al.* 1984; Paul *et al.* 1984) have investigated whether a correlation could be found between the percentage of cells with the fragile X activated or inactivated versus the mental status and the phenotypic expression in the heterozygous female. In some of these studies (Jacobs *et al.* 1980; Uchida and Joyce 1982; Knoll *et al.* 1984; Paul *et al.* 1984) the fragile X was found to be active more frequently than the normal X in mentally subnormal heterozygote females, and the opposite in the mentally normal. Other groups (Brøndum-Nielsen *et al.* 1983*b*; Fryns *et al.* 1984*a*) could not confirm these findings. Also, in a recent study of five other carriers we confirmed the previous findings. In these five moderate to high fragile X expressing female heterozygotes the fragile X was found to be active in most cells, varying from 57.9 per cent to 100 per cent of the informative cells, independent of IQ or phenotype. Thus, the present data seem to confirm that the mental status of carriers cannot be predicted by BrdU-inactivation studies, and indicate that there is no intrafamilial correlation of the fragile X inactivation as this was clearly different in three sisters of the same age-group and with the same mental level (Fryns and Van den Berghe 1988).

Evidence for an excess of twinning in families with the fragile X syndrome

Fragile X carriers have a high fertility, which is even higher in the mentally subnormal patients. An intriguing observation in our study of the progeny of 144 obligate carrier females was the high incidence of twinning. Of the 642 children, there were 18 pairs of twins. Of these, 12 were proven to be dizygotic; in six zygosity could not be determined. This incidence of twinning was high (1 in 35 births) and exceeded 3–4 times the expected incidence of twinning in Caucasians (1:80–1:140 births) (Fryns 1986). Sherman and Turner (1987) calculated the number of twin births among the total number of live births of known obligate carrier females found in fragile X families in New South Wales, Australia. They found that there were five male pairs, four female pairs, and nine unlike sex pairs of twins born among 752 births. Thus the twinning rate was 1/44 live births. This is a highly significant increase in twinning compared to the twinning rate of 1/96 live births in 1985 in New South Wales.

These observed two- to fourfold increases in twinning among fragile X carrier women is an important observation, and may be once more an indication for a dysregulation of the cortico-hypothalamo-hypophyseal axis in the fragile X syndrome.

Daughters of normal transmitting males

As discussed above, evidence for transmission of the fragile X chromosome through normal males has increasingly been observed. In contrast to the high incidence of mental subnormality and partial phenotypic expression (both ± 30 per cent) in female obligate carriers who inherited the fragile X chromosome from their mothers, mental and physical development is almost completely normal in all females who are carriers through their normal transmitting fathers. In those females, the fragile X site is difficult to demonstrate; in most of them fragile X screening is negative, and, in a few, we found extremely low percentages of fragile X positive cells. These daughters, as obligate heterozygotes, are at great risk of transmitting the marker to their children. These children can be mentally retarded and fragile X positive. To explain this phenomenon, Van Dyke and Weiss (1986) hypothesized a maternal effect on fragile X with variability in intelligence of heterozygotes and hemizygotes mediated mainly by the maternal uterus or placenta by virtue of different patterns of lyonization in those tissues between pregnancies. If the father contributes the fragile X, the intrauterine environment is invariably normal and so are the daughters. The ultimate phenotypes of the developing heterozygote and hemizygote may be determined by a threshold effect and interaction between the maternal genotype, the placental genotype, and the fetal genotype.

Pitfalls in prenatal diagnosis

Prenatal diagnosis

The high incidence of mental subnormality in female offspring of heterozygote carriers creates a difficult problem in genetic counselling. It indicates that prenatal diagnosis of the fragile X male does not remove the risk for the female heterozygote to have mentally retarded offspring (Schmidt *et al.* 1982; Webb *et al.* 1983). There is an insufficient correlation between the percentage of fragile X cells, the inactivation pattern of the fragile X, and the mental status of the individual female to solve this problem at present.

Technical difficulties in demonstrating the fragile X in amniotic cells or in cultures of chorionic villi are important, and failures have been reported resulting from low yields of marker X positive cells in amniocyte cultures. Negative and low-frequency positive results should be regarded with caution (Jenkins *et al.* 1987; Purvis-Smith *et al.* 1987; Shapiro *et al.* 1987; Tommerup *et al.* 1987). Further studies are clearly needed, to include fetal blood cultures and the use of restriction fragment length polymorphisms, to complement both pre- and postnatal fragile X diagnosis. This is especially important when the mutation is strongly suspected, though lymphocytes will probably turn out to be a more reliable source with regard to expression of the fragile X site. There are now several probes available for the genetic analysis of the fragile X syndrome but so far none of these is sufficiently closely linked to be of clinical use in pre- or postnatal diagnosis (see Brown, Chapter 4, this volume).

Fragile X screening programmes

Different genetic centres now have ten years' experience in large-scale fragile X screening programmes. At the present time it is evident that in the following groups of patients a fragile X screening is indicated as the first aetiological examination with absolute priority:

(1) familial mental retardation with borderline or mentally subnormal mother and multiple mentally retarded sibs, males and females;

(2) males of families with suspicion of X-linked mental retardation;

(3) fragile X screening in institutionalized mentally retarded males, and developmental disability in young males with hyperkinetic and/or autistic behaviour without gross dysmorphic or neurological symptoms.

In the group of familial mental retardation, a positive fragile X screening is found in 15–20 per cent of these families. Frequently, social and cultural deprivation was erroneously presumed to be the cause of the familial mental defect. The finding of a positive fragile X screening in these families is a definite indication that further research in these families will lead to a further diagnosis of other genetic and biological conditions, a *sine qua non* towards prevention and genetic counselling.

In 40–50 per cent of the families with suspicion of X-linked mental retardation on pedigree data, a fragile X syndrome is detected. This confirms that the fragile X syndrome represents less than 50 per cent of all forms of X-linked mental handicap.

Important differences exist in the percentages of fragile X males in different surveys on fragile X screening (Blomquist *et al.* 1982; Carpenter *et al.* 1982; Venter and Op't Hof 1982; Fishburn *et al.* 1983; Froster-Iskenius *et al.* 1983; Jacobs *et al.* 1983; Kähkönen *et al.* 1983; Brøndum-Nielsen *et al.* 1983*a*), but this is probably due to differences in selection criteria, e.g. more frequent institutionalization of patients who are severely retarded or manifest behavioural difficulties. In our study, a fragile X syndrome was detected in 16.1 per cent of the screened institutionalized male population, and in 2.9 per cent of the total population of mental retardation (Fryns *et al.* 1984*b*).

With regard to the criteria for fragile X screening in prepubertal patients, the recommendation can be made that a fragile X screening should be performed in all young male patients with psychomotor retardation of unknown aetiology, especially in those manifesting the characteristic behavioural problems of the fragile X male.

Under the direction of Gillian Turner, a preventive 3-year screening programme for the fragile X syndrome in the intellectually handicapped has been funded by the State Department of Health in New South Wales, Australia, in order to identify females at risk. This programme started 2 years ago, and is well accepted by the handicapped and their caretakers, and the majority of parents agree to the fragile X screening. Siblings are universally interested in the diagnosis and its consequences and request antenatal diagnosis. At the Troina Conference on X-linked mental retardation and fragile X, Gillian Turner concluded: 'By any standard the cost of the programme is small and the benefit great. We believe that now the omen is on health authorities to state why they are not screening for the fragile X.'

Other specific types of X-linked mental retardation

Introduction

As already discussed (p. 4) present data on X-linked mental retardation (*Proceedings of the Third International Workshop on the Fragile X and*

X-linked Mental Retardation 1988) screening is positive in no more than 40–50 per cent of all males with X-linked mental retardation.

During the past years an increasing number of clinically recognizable fragile X negative X-linked mental retardations have been delineated. Considering the other X-linked syndromes in which mental retardation can be associated (McKusick 1986), a total of 69 different entities have been reported until now. Some of them appear to be very rare; for most of them we do not know the incidence at birth.

At the Troina meeting (1987) on X-linked mental retardation and fragile X, Partington *et al.* (1987) reported a new type of X-linked mental retardation with athetoid spasms of the hands. In Table 1.3 we summarize our personal findings in this interesting field.

Table 1.3. X-linked mental retardation with clinical abnormalities

Disorder	Number of patients
Fragile X syndrome	465
Aarskog syndrome	42
Coffin–Lowry syndrome	11
Borjeson–Forssman–Lehmann syndrome	4
X-linked mental retardation with Marfanoid habitus	4
Atkin–Flaitz syndrome	2

Specific syndromes

The Aarskog syndrome (McKusick no. 30540)

At this moment the so-called 'facio-digito-genital syndrome' seems to be, after the fragile X syndrome, the most commom form of X-linked mental retardation (Aarskog 1970; Scott 1971; Furukawa *et al.* 1972; Sugarman *et al.* 1973; Berman *et al.* 1974; Fryns *et al.* 1978; Pedersen *et al.* 1980; Van den Bergh *et al.* 1984). The characteristic findings in this MCA syndrome are: short stature; flat face with short, upturned nose; triangular frontal hair implantation (widow's peak); triangular neck; genital hypoplasia with shawl scrotum; short hands and feet with interphalangeal webbing and hyperextensibility of the terminal phalanges of the hands (Fig. 1.13a–d). Most of these 'typical symptoms' disappear after puberty. The adult height is between 160 and 170 cm, the shawl scrotum is less evident after puberty, and testicular development is normal. In addition to the more or less unchanged morphology of the face, the hyperextensibility of the terminal phalanges is the only constant symptom in adult Aarskog males. The latter seems to be the most

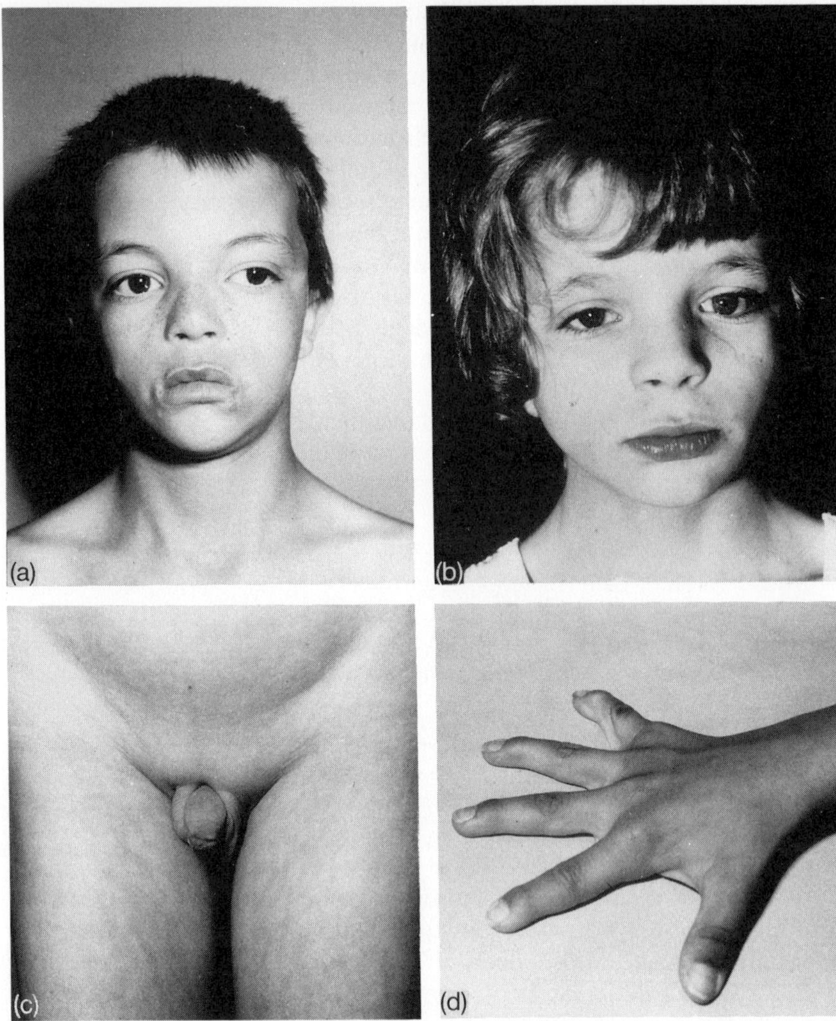

Fig. 1.13. The diagnostic clinical findings in Aarskog syndrome: (a) (b) the typical face; (c) the shawl scrotum; (d) the morphology of the hands.

reliable symptom in the differential diagnosis with Noonan syndrome, it is likely that Noonan males with hyperextensible distal phalanges are, in fact, examples of the Aarskog syndrome. A great clinical variability exists in the Aarskog syndrome, even within the same family; the developmental retardation is much more variable and never as serious as, for example, in Coffin–Lowry syndrome. In fact, 80 per cent of males with Aarskog syndrome are mentally normal and, moreover, in the mentally subnormal group more than two-thirds have IQs between 50 and 70 (Pedersen *et al.* 1980). The majority of female heterozygotes in the Aarskog syndrome are completely normal. Less than 20 per cent present some clinical features, most frequently a widow's peak or hyperextensible distal phalanges. Mental fitness is usually normal, and we personally know only two female heterozygotes with borderline intelligence (Van den Bergh *et al.* 1984).

The Coffin–Lowry syndrome (McKusick no. 30360)

After the original publication of Coffin *et al.* (1966) no more than 20 reports have dealt with this mental retardation syndrome, in which all males so far reported are severely mentally retarded (Martinelli and Campailla 1969; Lowry *et al.* 1971; Procopis and Turner 1972; Jammes *et al.* 1973; Temtamy *et al.* 1975; Fryns *et al.* 1977; Haspeslagh *et al.* 1984; Vles *et al.* 1984). They present with a typical clinical picture characterized by facial, hand, and skeletal anomalies. In adult males the facial features are diagnostic (Fig. 1.14a, b). The most salient features are: a broad quadrangular forehead with prominent supra-orbital ridges and heavy arched eyebrows, hypertelorism with antimongoloid slanting of the palpebral fissures and ptosis of the eyelids, a big nose with thick septum, a large open mouth with protruding tongue, irregular or missing teeth, big everted lips, and large everted ears. The large soft hands with thick lax skin and puffy tapering fingers can be diagnostic since they are never found in other mental retardation syndromes. Dermatoglyphic studies consistently show a transverse hypothenar crease. The most frequent and salient skeletal changes are thickened calvaria, spinal kyphosis and scoliosis with dysplasia of the vertebral bodies at the

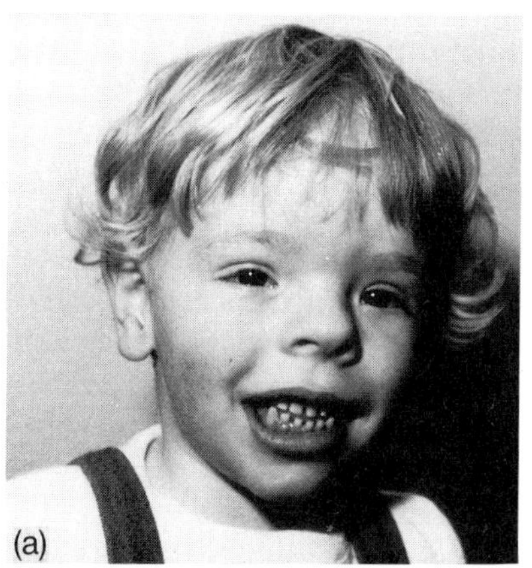
(a)

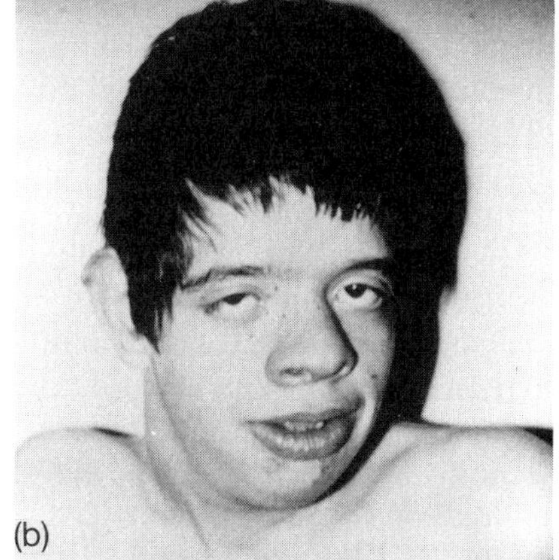
(b)

Fig. 1.14. Typical facial features in Coffin–Lowry syndrome.

thoracolumbar function, hypoplastic drum-stick type terminal phalanges, and retarded bone age. Other less constant changes include pectus carinatum or excavatum, cervical ribs, narrow iliac wings, and shortening of the long bones of the lower limbs. The diagnosis in infancy is much more difficult. The face is less dysmorphic, the coarseness only appears with age. At birth these children are hypotonic with hyperlaxity of joints. The early onset of internal hydrocephaly is probably responsible for the major neurological symptoms in these children (Vles *et al.* 1984). Soon after birth they present with a severe developmental delay and retarded bone age. Tapering fingers are present at birth and seem to be the most reliable feature in infancy. In contrast to the male patients, the clinical expression in females is variable, sometimes overlapping with a nearly normal phenotype (Haspeslagh *et al.* 1984). Besides the reduced mental fitness (80 per cent of patients) and the variable facial changes, tapering fingers (90 per cent) and short stature (75 per cent less than 160 cm) are the most constant findings in the female patients. According to present knowledge, it seems evident that some of the obligate female carriers are mentally normal and do not present facial or limb anomalies.

Borjeson–Forssman–Lehmann syndrome (McKusick no. 30190)

In 1962 Borjeson, Forssman, and Lehmann reported a new dysmorphic mental retardation syndrome in three related males. Until now, seven other authors have reported patients with this condition (for review see Dereymaeker *et al.* 1986). In addition to severe mental retardation, all patients have a history of seizures and present relative microcephaly, a plethoric fatty face with large, normally lobulated ears, obesity, hypogonadism, and short stature (Fig. 1.15). All males with this type of X-linked mental retardation are extremely aggressive and hyperkinetic. The underlying endocrine abnormality responsible for the postpubertal hypogonadism in this syndrome still remains obscure. Until now, both hypothalamic (Baar and Galindo 1965; Brun *et al.* 1974) and primary gonadal insufficiency (Weber *et al.* 1978) have been postulated.

X-linked mental retardation with Marfanoid habitus

Lujan *et al.* (1984) suggested the existence of a new X-linked mental retardation entity, in which Marfanoid habitus, peculiar facial appearance with large head and contrasting long and narrow face, and hypernasal voice seemed to be the three cardinal features. Recently we observed strikingly similar clinical abnormalities in two pairs of brothers (Fryns and Buttiens 1987). In all four males we had the clinical impression of an ectomorphic, Marfanoid habitus (Fig. 1.16a, b): difference between height and span; apparently long, slender fingers and toes; pectus excavatum; and hyperkyphosis. On clinical examination the

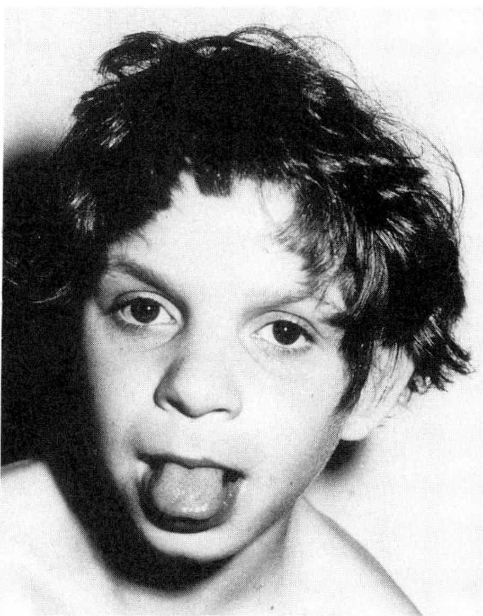

Fig. 1.15. The plethoric, fatty face in Borjeson–Forssman–Lehmann syndrome.

parents and mentally normal sibs were found to be normal, and the Marfanoid habitus was not a family trait in either family. It was only present in the mentally retarded males, and we could not find partial clinical expression of the apparently X-linked condition in female heterozygotes.

Macrocephaly, coarse facial features and short stature: the Atkin–Flaitz syndrome

In 1985 Atkin *et al.* were the first to describe a new, apparently X-linked mental retardation syndrome. In several members of a large family they found mental retardation and macrocephaly, associated with short stature and coarse facial features, including prominent forehead and heavy supraorbital ridges, hypertelorism, broad nasal tip with anteverted nostrils and thick lips. Recently, Clark and Baraitser (1987) reported a variant example of this apparently rare familial mental retardation syndrome. We had the opportunity to study another family with three severely affected sisters (Fryns *et al.* 1988*a*) (Fig. 1.17). It is interesting to note that the association of macrocephaly and mental retardation has previously been reported in a number of well-defined syndromes, i.e. cerebral gigantism and the fragile X-syndrome. Reviewing the literature, we have been impressed by two mentally retarded brothers reported by

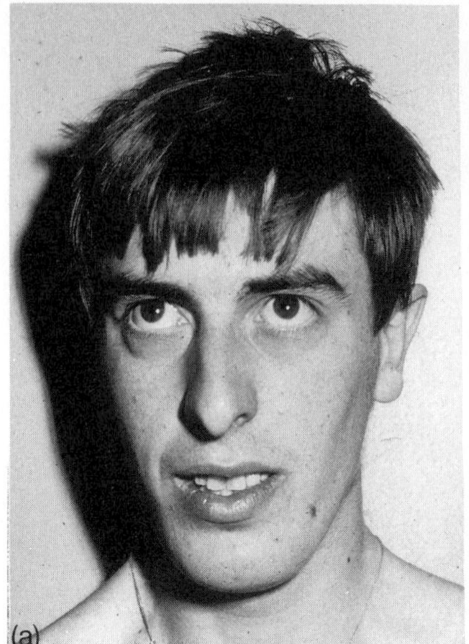

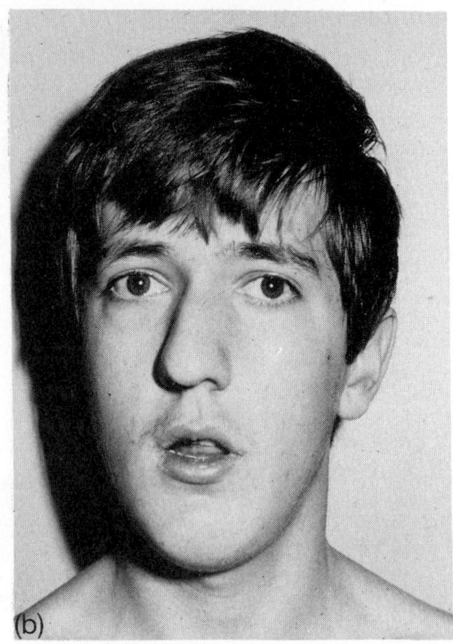

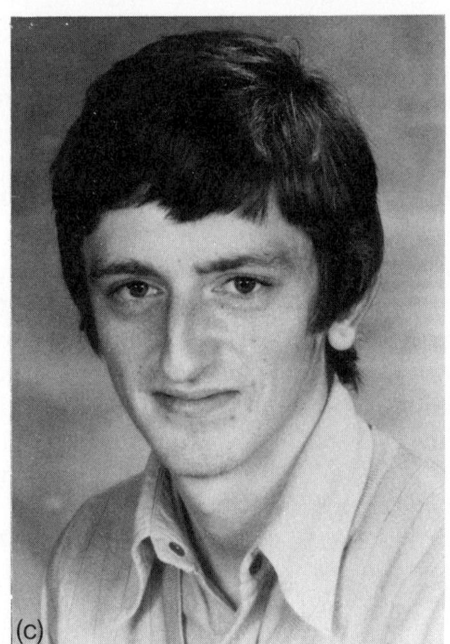

Fig. 1.16. Ectomorphic, Marfanoid habitus with peculiar face.

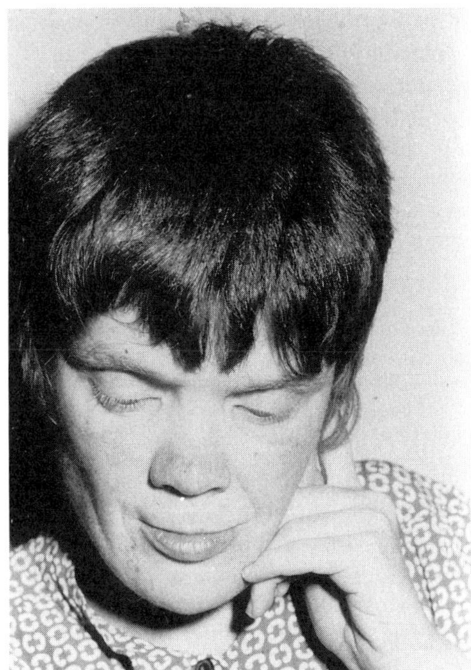

Fig. 1.17. Macrocephaly and coarse face in the Atkin–Flaitz syndrome.

Gragg in 1971, who presented an impressive megalocephaly and an almost identical facial coarseness. Golabi and Rosen (1984) reported a family in which four males in four sibships in three generations connected through females had macrocephaly and pre- and postnatal overgrowth. They presented, in addition, a MCA syndrome with facial dysmorphism, submucous cleft palate, 13 ribs, intestinal malrotation, coccygeal skin tag and bony appendage, and hand and feet anomalies with hypoplastic index finger nails and postaxial polydactyly. The available data seem to indicate that in the group of macrocephaly–X-linked mental retardation a number of other entities such as the Atkin–Flaitz syndrome will be delineated by careful examination of a large number of mentally retarded males and their respective families.

Further approach of and perspectives in non-specific X-linked mental retardation

As has been extensively discussed in the two previous paragraphs on fragile X and on 'syndromatic' X-linked mental retardation, both groups represent together probably less than 50 per cent of all patients with X-linked mental retardation. This is illustrated in Table 1.4, which summarizes recent personal data on the nosology of X-linked mental retardation in an institutionalized population of 263 severely and moderately mentally retarded patients of the Borgerstein Institute. In this study 11 of the 27 index patients with pedigree data compatible with X-linked inheritance were fragile X negative and had a non-syndromatic phenotype.

Table 1.4. The nosology of X-linked mental retardation in an institutionalized population of 263 patients

Type of diagnosis*	Number of index patients
Fragile X syndrome (30950)	11
Albright osteodystrophy (30080)	3
Coffin–Lowry syndrome (30360)	2
Aarskog syndrome (30540)	1
Acquired fragile X phenotype	3
Pedigree data compatible with X-linked mental retardation—fragile X negative	11

One of the major tasks for the near future will be to subdivide this hitherto unspecified group into further separate entities with the help of molecular biology and linkage studies. Recently, Sutherland *et al.* (1987) mapped the gene for one form of X-linked mental retardation (with short stature and microcephaly) provisionally close to the DXYS1 probe.

An intriguing observation in the group of the fragile X negative, clinically non-specific patients is the frequent finding of macrocephaly, associated with macro-orchidism in about half of them (see Table 1.5). An important question to be resolved in the next months and years is whether the genes for these 'macrocephalic' forms of X-linked mental retardation are in the same region as the fragile X mutation. As in the fragile X families, a constant finding in the hitherto non-specific forms is the high incidence of partial expression, at the mental and/or physical level, in carrier females (see Table 1.5). This problem will remain in the near future one of the most difficult questions for all families concerned with this problem and for all professionals working in this exciting field.

References

Aarskog, D. (1970). A familial syndrome of short stature associated with facial dysplasia and genital anomalies. *Journal of Pediatrics*, **77**, 856–60.

Table 1.5. Clinical data in index patients of 11 fragile X negative families with pedigree data compatible with X-linked inheritance

Family number	1.	2	3	4*		5	6	7	8	9	10	11
Index patients												
Sex	male	male	male	female	male	male	male	male	male	male	male	male
Moderate mental retardation	+	+		+	+	slight	+	+	+	+	+	+
Macrocephaly	+	+	–	+	+	+	+	+	–	+	–	–
Large ears	+	–	–	–	–	–	–	–	–	–	–	–
Long face	+	–	–	+	+	–	–	–	–	–	–	–
Large testes	+	+	–			+	+	–	–	+	–	+
Others	–	–	–	–	–	maxillary hypoplasia	large hands and feet	hypogonadism obesity	–	–	–	facial oedema
Mother												
Facial features	+	?	–	?	?	–	–	–	?	–	–	
Borderline intelligence to slight mental retardation	+	+	+	?	+	+	+	+	?	–	–	

*Brother and sister institutionalized in the same institute.

Allan, W. H., Herndon, C. N., and Dudley, F. C. (1944). Some examples of the inheritance of mental deficiency: apparently sex-linked idiocy and microcephaly. *American Journal of Mental Deficiencies,* **48**, 325–34.

Atkin, J. F., Flaitz, K., Patil, S., and Smith, W. (1985). A new X-linked mental retardation syndrome. *American Journal of Medical Genetics,* **21**, 697–705.

Baar, H. S. and Galindo, J. (1965). The Borjeson–Forssman–Lehmann syndrome. *Journal of Mental Deficiency Research,* **9**, 125–30.

Beemer, F. A., Veenema, H., and de Pater, J. M. (1986). Cerebral gigantism (Sotos syndrome) in two patients with fra(X) chromosomes. *American Journal of Medical Genetics. Special issue: X-linked mental retardation 2,* **23**, 221–6.

Bergh, P. van den, Fryns, J. P., Wilms, G., Piot, R., Dralands, G., and Van den Bergh, R. (1984). Anomalous cerebral venous drainage in Aarskog syndrome. *Clinical Genetics,* **25**, 288–94.

Berman, P., Desjardins, C., and Fraser, F. C. (1974). Inheritance of the Aarskog syndrome. *Birth defects: original article series malformation syndromes* **X/7**, pp. 151–60. The National Foundation, March of Dimes, The Williams & Wilkins Company, Baltimore.

Blomquist, H. K., Gustavson, K. H., Holmgren, G., Nordenson, I., and Sweins, A. (1982). Fragile site X chromosomes and X-linked mental retardation in severely retarded boys in a Northern Swedish county. A prevalance study. *Clinical Genetics,* **21**, 209–14.

Blomquist, H. K., Gustavson, K. H., Holmgren, G., Nordenson, I., and Pălsson-Straĕ, U. (1983). Fragile X sydrome in mildly mentally retarded children in a Northern Swedish county. A prevalence study. *Clinical Genetics,* **24**, 393–8.

Borghgraef, M., Fryns, J. P., Dielkens, A., Pyck, K., and Van den Berghe, H. (1987). Fragile(X) syndrome: a study of the psychological profile in 23 prepubertal patients. *Clincal Genetics,* **32**, 179–86.

Brøndum-Nielsen, K., Dyggve, H. V., Knuden, H., and Olsen, J. (1983*a*). A chromosomal survey of an institution for mentally retarded . *Danish Medical Bulletin,* **30**, 5–13.

Brøndum-Nielsen, K., Tommerup, N., Poulsen, H., Jacobsen, P., Beck, B., and Mikkelsen, M. (1983*b*). Carrier detection and X-inactivation studies in the fragile X syndrome. Cytogenetic studies in 63 obligate and potential carriers of the fragile X. *Human Genetics,* **64**, 240–5.

Brun, A., Borjeson, M., and Forssman, H. (1974). An inherited syndrome with mental deficiency and endocrine disorder. A patho-anatomical study. *Journal of Mental Deficiency Research,* **18**, 317.

Bundey, S. and Carter, C. O. (1974). Recurrence risks in severe undiagnosed mental deficiency. *Journal of Mental Deficiency Research,* **18**, 115–34.

Carpenter, N. J. (1983). The fragile X chromosome and its clinical manifestation. In *Cytogenetics of the mammalian X chromosome,* Part B, (ed. A. Sandberg), pp. 399–414. Alan R. Liss, New York.

Carpenter, N. J., Leichtman, L. G., and Say, B. (1982). Fragile X-linked mental retardation. A survey of 65 patients with mental retardation of unknown origin. *American Journal of Diseases of Children,* **136**, 392–8.

Christian, J. C., Demeyers, W., Franken, E. A., Huff, J. S., Khairl, S., and Reed, T.

(1977). X-linked skeletal dysplasia with mental retardation. *Clinical Genetics*, **11**, 128–36.

Clark, R. D. and Baraitser, M. (1987). Letter to the editor. A new X-linked mental retardation syndrome. *American Journal of Medical Genetics*, **26**, 13–15.

Coffin, G. S., Siris, E., and Wegienka, L. C. (1966). Mental retardation with osteocartilagenous anomalies. *American Journal of Diseases of Children*, **112**, 205–13.

Dereymaeker, A. M., Fryns, J. P., Hoefnagels, M., Heremans, G., Marien, J., and Van den Berghe, H. (1986). The Borjeson–Forssman–Lehmann syndrome. A family study. *Clinical Genetics* **29**, 317–20.

Dunn, H. G., Renpenning, H., Gerrard, J. W., Miller, J. R., Tabata, T., and Fedoroff, S. (1963). Mental retardation as a sex-linked defect. *American Journal of Mental Deficiencies*, **67**, 827–48.

Dyke, D. L. van and Weiss, L. (1986). Maternal effect on intelligence in fragile X males and females. *American Journal of Medical Genetics, Special issue: X-linked mental retardation 2*, **23**, 723–37.

Engel, E. (1983). L'arriération mentale avec fragilité de l'X: Armenfrax. Revue et études personelles. *Revue Médicale de la Suisse Romande*, **103**, 333–44.

Escalanté, J. A., Grunspun, H., and Fronta Pessoa, O. (1971). Severe sexlinked mental retardation. *Journal de Génétique Humaine*, **19**, 137–40.

Fishburn, J., Turner, G., Daniel, A., and Brookwell, R. (1983). The diagnosis and frequency of X-linked conditions in a cohort of moderately retarded males with affected brothers. *American Journal of Medical Genetics*, **14**, 713–24.

Fried, K. (1972). X-linked mental retardation and/or hydrocephalus. *Clinical Genetics*, **3**, 258–63.

Froster-Iskenius, U., Schwinger, E., Weigert, M., and Fonatsch, C. (1982). Replication pattern in XXY cells with fra(X). *Human Genetics*, **60**, 278–80.

Froster-Iskenius, U., Felsch, G., Schirren, C., and Schwinger, E. (1983). Screening for fra(X)(q) in a population of mentally retarded males. *Human Genetics*, **63**, 153–7.

Froster-Iskenius, U., Bodeker, K., Oepen, T., Matthes, R., Piper, U., and Schwinger, E. (1986). Folic acid treatment in males and females with fragile-(X)-syndrome. *Americal Journal of Medical Genetics, Special Issue: X-linked mental retardation 2*, **23**, 273–89.

Fryns, J. P. (1984). The fragile X syndrome. A study of 83 families. *Clinical Genetics*, **26**, 497–528.

Fryns, J. P. (1986). The female and the fragile X. A study of 144 obligate female carriers. *American Journal of Medical Genetics*, **23**, 157–69.

Fryns, J. P. and Buttiens, M. (1987). X-linked mental retardation with Marfanoid habitus. *American Journal of Medical Genetics*, **28**, 267–74.

Fryns, J. P. and Van den Berghe, H. (1982). Transmission of fragile (X)(q27) from normal male(s). *Human Genetics*, **61**, 262–3.

Fryns, J. P. and Van den Berghe, H. (1986). 8q24.12 interstitial deletion in trichorhinophalangeal syndrome type I. *Human Genetics*, **74**, 188–9.

Fryns, J. P. and Van den Berghe, H. (1988). Inactivation pattern of the fragile X in heterozygous carriers. Proceedings Third International Workshop on the

Fragile X and X-linked Mental Retardation. *American Journal of Medical Genetics*, **30**, 401–6.

Fryns, J. P., Vinken, L., and Van den Berghe, H. (1977). The Coffin syndrome. *Human Genetics*, **36**, 271–6.

Fryns, J. P., Macken, J., Vinken, L., Igodt-Ameye, L., and Van den Berghe, H. (1978). The Aarskog syndrome. *Human Genetics*, **42**, 129–35.

Fryns, J. P. *et al.* (1983). XY/XXY mosaicism and fragile X syndrome. *Annales de Génétique*, **26**, 251–3.

Fryns, J. P., Kleczkowska, A., Kubień, E., Petit, P., and Van de Berghe, H. (1984*a*). Inactivation pattern of the fragile X in heterozygous carriers. *Human Genetics*, **65**, 400–1.

Fryns, J. P., Kleczkowska, A., Kubień, E., and Van den Berghe, H. (1984*b*). Cytogenetic findings in moderate and severe mental retardation. A study of an institutionalized population of 1991 patients. *Acta Paediatrica Scandinavica*, Supplement 313.

Fryns, J. P., Kleczkowska, A., Wolfs, I., and Van den Berghe, H. (1984*c*). Klinefelter syndrome and two fragile X chromosomes. *Clinical Genetics*, **26**, 445–7.

Fryns, J. P., Dereymaeker, A. M., Haegeman, J., and Van den Berghe, H. (1988*a*). Mental retardation, macrocephaly, short stature and craniofacial dysmorphism in three sisters. A new entity among the mental retardation–macrocephaly syndromes? *Clinical Genetics*, **33**, 293–8.

Fryns, J. P., Haspeslagh, M., Dereymaeker, A. M., Volcke, Ph., and Van den Berghe, H. (1988*b*). A peculiar subphenotype in the fra(X) syndrome: Extreme obesity—short stature—stubby hands and feet—diffuse hyperpigmentation. Another evidence of disturbed hypothalamic function in the fra(X) syndrome? *Clinical Genetics*, **32**, 388–92.

Fryns, J. P., Moerman, P., Gills, F., D'Espallier, L., and Van den Berghe, H. (1988*c*). Suggestively increased rate of infant death in children of fra(X) positive mothers. Proceedings Third International Workshop on the Fragile X and X-linked Mental Retardation. *American Journal of Medical Genetics*, **30**, 73–5.

Furukawa, C. T., Hall, B. D., and Smith, D. W. (1972). The Aarskog syndrome, *Journal of Pediatrics*, **81**, 1117–22.

Goddard, H. H. (1914). *Feeblemindedness. Its causes and consequences.* MacMillan, New York.

Golabi, M., and Rosen, L. (1984). A new X-linked mental retardation-overgrowth syndrome. *American Journal of Medical Genetics*, **17**, 345–58.

Gragg, G. W. (1971). Familial megalencephaly. *Birth Defects: Original Article Series*, **VII**, (1), 228–9.

Grouchy, J. de and Turleau, C. (1977). *Atlas des maladies Chromosomiques*, pp. 98–105. Expansion Scientifique, Paris.

Haspeslagh, M., Fryns, J. P., Beusen, L., Van Dessel, F., Vinken, L., and Van den Berghe, H. (1984). The Coffin–Lowry syndrome. A study of two new index patients and their families. *European Journal of Pediatrics*, **143**, 82–86.

Hawkey, C. J. and Smithies, A. (1976). The Prader–Willi syndrome with a 15/15 translocation. *Journal of Medical Genetics*, **13**, 152–63.

Herbst, D. S. (1980). Nonspecific X-linked mental retardation. I: A review with information from 24 new families. *American Journal of Medical Genetics*, **7**, 443–60.

Herbst, D. S. and Miller, J. R. (1980). Nonspecific X-linked mental retardation. II. The frequency in British Columbia. *American Journal of Medical Genetics*, **7**, 461–9.

Herbst, D. S., Dunn, H. G., Dill, F. J., Kalousek, D. K., and Krywaniuk, L. W. (1981). Further delineation of X-linked mental retardation. *Human Genetics*, **58**, 366–72.

Jacobs, P. A., *et al.* (1980). X-linked mental retardation: a study of 7 families. *American Journal of Medical Genetics*, **7**, 471–89.

Jacobs, P. A., Mayer, M., Matsuura, J., Rhoads, F., and Yee, S. C. (1983). A cytogenetic study of a population of mentally retarded males with special reference to the marker (X) syndrome. *Human Genetics*, **63**, 139–48.

Jammes, J., Mirhoseini, S. A., and Holmes, L. B. (1973). Syndrome of facial abnormalities, kyphoscoliosis and severe mental retardation. *Clinical Genetics*, **4**, 203–9.

Jenkins, E. C. *et al.* (1987). *Recent experience in prenatal fra(X) detection.* Abstracts, Third International Workshop on the Fragile X and X-linked Mental Retardation. Troina, 13–16 September.

Jennings, M., Hall, J. G., and Hoehn, H., (1980). Significance of phenotypic and chromosomal abnormalities in X-linked mental retardation (Martin–Bell or Renpenning syndrome). *American Journal of Medical Genetics*, **7**, 417–32.

Johnson, G. E. (1897). Contribution to the psychology and pedagogy of feebleminded children. *Journal of Psycho-Astenics*, **2**, 26–32.

Kähkönen, M., Leisti, J., Wilska, M., and Varonen, S. (1983). Marker X-associated mental retardation. A study of 150 retarded males. *Clinical Genetics*, **23**, 397–404.

Kemper, M. B., Hagerman, R. J., Ahmad, R. S., and Mariner, R. (1986). Cognitive profiles and the spectrum of clinical manifestations in heterozygous fra(X) females. *American Journal of Medical Genetics, Special Issue: X-linked mental retardation 2*, **23**, 139–56.

Knoll, J. H., Chudley, A. E., and Gerrard, J. W. (1984). Fragile (X) X-linked mental retardation. II. Frequency and replication pattern of fragile (X)(q28) in heterozygotes. *American Journal of Human Genetics*, **36**, 640–5.

Lehrke, R. (1972). A theory of X-linkage of major intellectual traits. *American Journal of Mental Deficiencies*, **76**, 611–19.

Lehrke, R. (1974). X-linked mental retardation and verbal disability. *Birth Defects, Original Article Series* **X**, (1), 1–100.

Loehr, J. P., Synhorst, D. P., Wolfe, R. R., and Hagerman, R. J. (1986). Aortic root dilatation and mitral valve prolapse in the fragile X syndrome. *American Journal of Medical Genetics*, **23**, 189–94.

Lowry, B., Miller, J. R., and Fraser, F. C. (1971). A new dominant gene mental retardation syndrome. *American Journal of Diseases of Children*, **121**, 496–500.

Lubs, H. A. (1969). A marker X-chromosome. *American Journal of Human Genetics*, **21**, 231–44.

Lujan, J. E., Carlis, M. E., Lubs, H. A. (1984). A form of X-linked mental retardation with marfanoid habitus. *American Journal of Medical Genetics*, **17**, 311–22.

Martin, J. P. and Bell, J. (1943). A pedigree of mental defect showing sex-linkage. *Journal of Neurological Psychiatry*, **6**, 154–7.

Martinelli, B. and Campailla, E. (1969). Contribute alla consoscenze della sindrome di Coffin. *Psychiatria et Neurologica (Basel)*, **97**, 449.

Mattei, J. F., Mattei, M. G., Aumeras, C., Auger, M., and Giraud, F. (1981). X-linked mental retardation with the fragile X. A study of 15 families. *Human Genetics*, **59**, 281–9.

McKusick, V. A. (1986). *Mendelian inheritance in man. Catalogs of autosomal, dominant, autosomal recessive, and X-linked phenotypes*, (7th edn). The Johns Hopkins University Press, Baltimore.

Meryash, D. L., Cronk, C. E., Sachs, B., and Gerald, P. S. (1984). An anthropometric study of males with the fragile X syndrome. *American Journal of Medical Genetics*, **17**, 159–74.

Musumeci, S. A. *et. al.* (1987). *Prevalence of a novel epileptogenic EEG pattern in fragile-X syndrome.* Abstracts, Third International Workshop on the Fragile X and X-linked Mental Retardation. Troina, 13–16 September.

Neuhäuser, G., Zerbin-Rüdin, E., Pfeiffer, R. A. and Klar, H. (1969). Beobachtung zum Problem des geschlechtsgebunden-rezessiven Schwachsinss. *Archiv für Psychiatrie und Nervenkraukheiten*, **212**, 207–24.

Opitz, J. M., Segal, A. T., Klove, H., Matthews, Ch., and Lehrke, R. C. (1965). X-linked mental retardation. A study of a large kindred with 20 affected members. *Journal of Pediatrics*, **67**, 713–14.

Opitz, J. M. and Sutherland, G. R. (1984). Conference Report: International workshop on the fragile X and X-linked mental retardation. *American Journal of Medical Genetics*, **17**, 5–94.

Partington, M. W. (1986). Invited editorial comment: X-linked Mental Retardation: Caveats in genetic counselling. *American Journal of Medical Genetics, Special issue: X-linked mental retardation 2*, **23**, 101–9.

Partington, M. W., Hockey, A., Sutherland, G. R., Mulley, J. C., Thode, A., and Turner, G. (1987). *X-linked mental retardation with athetoid spasms of the hands.* Abstracts, Third International Workshop on the Fragile X and X-linked Mental Retardation. Troina, 13–16 September.

Paul, J., Froster-Iskenius, U., Moje, W., and Schwinger, E. (1984). Heterozygous female carriers of the marker-X-chromosome: IQ estimation and replication status of fra(X)(q). *Human Genetics*, **66**, 344–6.

Pedersen, J. C., Fryns, J. P., Bracke, P., Geeraert, M., and Van den Berghe, H. (1980). The Aarskog syndrome. *Annales de Génétique* **23**, 108–10.

Penrose, L. S. (1938). *A clinical and genetic study of 1280 cases of mental defect.* Medical Research Council. Special Report Series no. 229.

Priest, J. H., Thulline, H. C., La Veck, F. G., and Jarvis, D. B. (1961). An approach to genetic factors in mental retardation. *American Journal of Mental Deficiencies*, **66**, 42–50.

Proceedings of the Third International Workshop on the Fragile X and X-linked Mental Retardation (1988). Troina, 13–16 September, 1987. *American*

Journal of Medical Genetics, in press.

Procopis, P. G. and Turner, B. (1972). Mental retardation, abnormal fingers and skeletal anomalies: Coffin's syndrome. *American Journal of Diseases of Children*, **124**, 258–61.

Purvis-Smith, S., Laing, S., and Sutherland, G. R. (1987). *Prenatal diagnosis of fragile X—the Australasian experience.* Abstracts, Third International Workshop on the Fragile X and X-linked Mental Retardation. Troina, 13–16 September.

Reed, E. W. and Reed, S. C. (1965). *Mental retardation: a family study.* W. B. Saunders, Philadelphia.

Renpenning, H. J., Gerrard, J. W., Zaleski, W. A., and Tabata, T. (1963). Familial sex-linked mental retardation. *Canadian Medical Association Journal*, **87**, 954–6.

Schmidt, A., Passarge, E., Seemanová, E., and Macek, M. (1982). Prenatal detection of a fetus hemizygous for the fragile X-chromosome. *Human Genetics*, **62**, 285–6.

Schönenberg, H. and Böttcher, B. (1974). Geschlechtsgebunden rezessiv vererbe Oligophrenie. *Medizinische Klinik*, **69**, 1814–16.

Scott, C. I. (1971). Unusual facies, joint hypermobility, genital anomaly and short stature: A new dysmorphic syndrome. *Birth Defects: Original Article Series*, **VII/6**, 240–6.

Shapiro, L. R., Wilmot, P. L., Murphy, P. D., and Breg, W. R. (1987). *Experience with multiple approaches to the prenatal diagnosis of the fragile X syndrome: amniotic fluid, chorionic villi, fetal blood and molecular methods.* Abstracts, Third International Workshop on the Fragile X and X-linked Mental Retardation. Troina, 13–16 September.

Sherman, S. L. and Turner, G. (1987). *Evidence for an excess of twinning in families with the fragile X syndrome.* Abstracts, Third International Workshop on the Fragile X and X-linked Mental Retardation. Troina, 13–16 September.

Sherman, S. L., Morton, N. E., Jacobs, P. A., and Turner, G. (1984). The marker (X) syndrome: a cytogenetic and genetic analysis. *Annals of Human Genetics*, **48**, 21–37.

Smith, D. W. (1982). *Major problems in clinical pediatrics.* Vol. VII. *Recognizable patterns of human malformation. Genetic, embryologic and clinical aspects.* W. B. Saunders, Philadelphia.

Snyder, R. D. and Robinson, A. (1969). Recessive sex-linked mental retardation in the absence of other recognizable abnormalities. *Clinical Pediatrics, (Phila)*, **8**, 669–74.

Steele, M. W. and Chorazy, A. L. (1974). Renpenning's syndromes. *Lancet*, **i**, (2), 752–3.

Sugarman, G. I., Rimoin, D. L., and Lachman, R. S. (1973). The facial-digital-genital (Aarskog) syndrome. *American Journal of Diseases of Children*, **126**, 248–52.

Sutherland, G. R. (1977). Fragile sites on human chromosomes: demonstration of their dependence on the type of tissue culture medium. *Science*, **197**, 265–6.

Sutherland, G. R. and Ashforth, P. L. C. (1979). X-linked mental retardation with macroorchidism and the fragile site at Xq27 or 28. *Human Genetics,* **48**, 117–20.

Sutherland, G. R., Gedeon, A. K., Haan, E. A., and Mulley, J. C. (1987). *The gene for one form of X-linked mental retardation is closely linked to DXYS1.* Abstracts, Third International Workshop on the Fragile X and X-linked Mental Retardation. Troina, 13–16 September.

Temtamy, S. A. *et al.* (1975). The Coffin–Lowry syndrome. A single inherited trait comprising mental retardation, facial digital anomalies and skeletal involvement. *Birth Defects: Original Article Series* **XI**, (6), 133–52.

Tommerup, N. *et al.* (1987). *First trimester prenatal diagnosis of the fragile site at Xq27.* Abstracts, Third International Workshop on the Fragile X and X-linked Mental Retardation. Troina, 13–16 September.

Turner, G. and Opitz, J. M. (1980). Editorial comment: X-linked mental retardation. *American Journal of Medical Genetics,* **7**, 407–15.

Turner, G. and Partington, M. W. (1987). *The correlation between fragile X expression and degree of intellectual handicap in the male.* Abstracts, Third International Workshop on the Fragile X and X-linked Mental Retardation. Troina, 13–16 September.

Turner, G. and Turner, B. (1974). X-linked mental retardation. *Journal of Medical Genetics,* **11**, 109.

Turner, G., Eastman, C., Casev, J., McLeav, A., Procopis, P., and Turner, B. (1975). Mental retardation with bilateral enlargement of the testes without any endocrinological disturbance. *Journal of Medical Genetics,* **12**, 367–71.

Turner, G., Daniel, A., and Frost, M. (1980). X-linked mental retardation macro-orchidism, and the Xq27 fragile site. *Journal of Pediatrics,* **96**, 837–41.

Turner, G. *et al.* (1986). Conference Report: Second international workshop on the fragile X and on X-linked mental retardation. *American Journal of Medical Genetics,* **23**, 11–67.

Uchida, I. A. and Joyce, E. M. (1982). Activity of the fragile X in heterozygous carriers. *American Journal of Human Genetics,* **34**, 286–93.

Venter, P. A. and Op't Hof, J. (1982). Cytogenetic abnormalities including the marker X chromosome in patients with severe mental retardation. *South African Medical Journal,* **62**, 947–50.

Venter, P. A., Op't Hof, J., and Coetzee, D. J. (1986). The Martin–Bell syndrome in South Africa. *American Journal of Medical Genetics, Special Issue: X-linked mental retardation 2,* **23**, 597–610.

Vles, J. S. H., Haspeslagh, M., Raes, M. M. R., Fryns, J. P., Casaer, P., and Eggermont, E. (1984). Early clinical signs in Coffin–Lowry syndrome. *Clinical Genetics,* **26**, 448–52.

Waldstein, G., Dawson, D. L., Hagerman, R., Mierau, R., and Thibodeau, S. (1987). *Aortic hypoplasia and elastin abnormalities in a male with Fragile X syndrome.* Abstracts, Third International Workshop on the Fragile X and X-linked Mental Retardation. Troina, 13–16 September.

Walker, F. A. (1973). Three new apparent X-linked entities. *Genetics,* **74**, 288–9.

Webb, G. C., Rogers, I. G., Pitt, D. B., Halliday, J., and Theobald, T. (1981). Transmission of fragile(X)(q27) site from a male. *Lancet,* **i**, 1231–2.

Webb, T., Gosden, C. M., Rodeck, C. H., Hamill, M. A., and Eason, P. E. (1983).

Prenatal diagnosis of X-linked mental retardation with fragile(X) using fetoscopy and fetal blood sampling. *Prenatal Diagnosis*, **3**, 131–7.

Weber, F. T., Frias, J. L., Julius, R. L., and Felman, A. H. (1978). Primary hypogonadism in the Borjeson–Forssman–Lehmann syndrome. *Journal of Medical Genetics,* **15**, 63.

Wilmot, P. L., Shapiro, L., and Duncan, P. A. (1980). The Xq27 fragile site and 47,XXY. *American Journal of Human Genetics,* **32**, 94A (Suppl.).

Yarbrough, K. M. and Howard-Peebles, P. N. (1976). X-linked non-specific mental retardation: report of a large kindred. *Clinical Genetics*, **10**, 125–30.

2 The epidemiology of the fragile X syndrome

TESSA WEBB

Introduction

There are several different ways of approaching the epidemiology of the fragile X syndrome. One of the most difficult parameters to obtain is that of total prevalence rate and hence gene frequency within a total population. Estimates of the contribution of the syndrome to the aetiology of mental handicap can be obtained more easily, and have been made by screening populations of retarded individuals for the presence of the fragile or marker X (fra Xq27).

Studies have also been carried out upon other defined groups of individuals who exhibit some of the criteria associated with the fragile X. Such criteria can include widely differing clinical manifestations, such as macro-orchidism or autistic behaviour. Although total surveys for the fragile X syndrome have not been widely reported within defined populations, the fragile X chromosome has been detected in all of the main ethnic groups.

Prevalence studies

A complete ascertainment of every individual who carries the marker or fragile X within a defined population has not yet been attempted. Apart from the problems involved in screening a large enough body of people to render the results meaningful, two-thirds of the female carriers are of normal intelligence and one-third do not demonstrate the cytogenetic marker at all and so can only be ascertained if they are obligate carriers. As approximately one-fifth of the fragile X males are also of normal intelligence and do not demonstrate the marker X (the transmitting males), even the most comprehensive prevalence studies have to be based upon the contribution of the syndrome to mental handicap and extrapolations made in order to calculate actual frequencies.

The total ascertainment of all mentally retarded individuals within a large population is difficult for two main reasons. First after school-age many subjects 'disappear' into the community, as often very little provision is made for handicapped adults; and, secondly, as mental handicap due to the presence of the fragile X syndrome may be only moderate or mild (particularly in girls), many affected children start off in normal primary schools and are only assessed as handicapped when they move to secondary school. The most accurate estimate of the contribution of the fragile X syndrome to mental handicap will therefore be made by ascertaining the prevalence of the condition in children attending secondary schools, generally those between 11 and 18 years of age.

An alternative approach to that of screening populations in order to find the frequency of X-linked mental retardation (XLMR) was taken by Herbst and Miller (1980) who estimated the frequency in Britsh Columbia by employing a health surveillance registry. They found, by extrapolating figures for the excess of brother–brother pairs over sister–sister pairs, that the frequency of XLMR was 1.83/1000 males. With the assumption that approximately one-third to a half of XLMR is due to the fragile X syndrome (Howard-Peebles and Stoddard 1980; Turner *et al.* 1980*b*; Herbst *et al.* 1981), the frequency of the fragile X syndrome becomes 0.92/1000 male births.

The excess of affected brother–brother over sister–sister pairs in the study of XLMR had been used previously by Priest *et al.* (1961) and by Turner and Turner (1974). Although some estimates are higher (Howard-Peebles 1982), in Australia Turner *et al.* (1970) found that XLMR accounted for about 10 per cent of moderate retardation in males, and, using this figure, in 1974 estimated a minimum prevalance of moderate XLMR equal to 0.56/1000 males. When this group was restudied later (Fishburn *et al.* 1983) it was calculated that 1.9/10 000 males were moderately retarded due to the fragile X syndrome but that 0.9/10 000 males had both macro-orchidism and mental retardation but were fragile X negative. These authors also found moderate XLMR to be more prevalent in rural rather than urban areas.

Several of the studies aimed at total ascertainment of all individuals with the fragile X syndrome have been carried out in Scandinavia. Gustavson *et al.* (1977) studying all children born in a northern Swedish county between 1959 and 1970 estimated that 8.1/1000 had IQ < 70. Of these children, 4.2/1000 were mildly mentally retarded, with IQ 50–69 (Blomquist *et al.* 1981). These authors then went on to study the contribution of the fragile X syndrome to mental handicap, finding that in Vasterbotten the incidence of the fragile X syndrome was 1/1500 or 0.67/1000 boys (Gustavson *et al.* 1986).

In the Kuopio province of Finland, mentally retarded children were ascertained not only by means of registers but also by employing school achievement tests. The fragile X syndrome was found to have a prevalence of 0.8/1000 males and 0.4/1000 females (Kähkönen *et al.* 1987).

In a possibly more ethnically mixed population resident in Coventry, UK, an attempt was made to ascertain the prevalance of the fragile X syndrome by studying children attending schools for the educationally subnormal. The prevalence in schoolboys was found to be 0.75/1000 and in schoolgirls 0.6/1000 (Webb *et al.* 1986).

A similar study carried out in New South Wales, with the aim of assessing the possibility of preventative screening for the syndrome, estimated that among educationally subnormal schoolchildren the prevalence of the fragile X was 0.4/1000 in males and 0.2/1000 in females (Turner *et al.* 1986).

In all of these studies a degree of selection was applied after the total number of retarded children was ascertained, and compliance ranged from 64–73 per cent in boys and 62–78 per cent in girls. Sherman *et al.* (1984), in a statistical analysis of data from many individual studies, estimated that for males the frequency of the marker X syndrome was 0.44/1000 and for females it was 0.41/1000, while in a comprehensive review of marker X linked mental retardation Turner and Jacobs (1983) estimated the frequency to be 1/2000 males.

Thus the estimate of total prevalence of the fragile X syndrome obtained mainly from populations of European extraction vary from 0.4/1000 to 0.9/1000 for males and 0.2/1000 to 0.6/1000 for females (Tables 2.1 and 2.2).

Table 2.1. Prevalence studies of the fragile X syndrome among males

Study	Location	Total number of males in the population	Total number of males studied	Prevalence of the fragile X syndrome
Gustavson *et al.* (1986)	Sweden	40 871	89	0.7/1000
Herbst and Miller (1980)	Canada			0.9/1000
Kähkönen *et al.* (1987)	Finland	6594	61	0.8/1000
Turner *et al.* (1986)	Australia	58 094	472	0.4/1000
Webb *et al.* (1986)	UK	28 611	219	0.7/1000

Selected populations

The many studies on selected populations have permitted estimates to be made of the contribution of the fragile X syndrome to morbidity. The most studied are the mentally handicapped, but screening for the marker

Table 2.2. Prevalence studies of the fragile X syndrome among females

Study	Location	Total number of females in the population	Total number of females studied	Prevalence of the fragile X syndrome
Kähkönen *et al.* (1987)	Finland	6288	50	0.4/1000
Turner *et al.* (1986)	Australia	56 641	203	0.2/1000
Webb *et al.* (1986)	UK	26 945	128	0.6/1000

X syndrome has been undertaken using this with several other selection criteria.

Mentally retarded populations

The main difficulty encountered in interpreting and comparing this type of survey is in the degree of selection applied to the individuals within each study. Thus, some make no attempt to define their population, selecting for mental handicap alone; while others may define the level of handicap, still others may consider only those with retardation of unknown aetiology, and others consider only those with no dysmorphic features or neurological signs.

In Sweden, studies have been performed on severely mentally retarded children, where among 96 boys with IQ < 50, 6 per cent had the fragile X (Blomquist *et al.* 1982); and in mildly mentally retarded children with IQ 50–70, where among 110 boys 4.5 per cent had the fragile X but among 61 girls not one did (Blomquist *et al.* 1983). Overall, in an unselected group of children with IQ < 70, 12/75 or 5.9 per cent of the boys had the marker X. When only those with no known diagnosis for their retardation were considered then 12/89 or 13.5 per cent of the boys were marker X positive.

A study of mentally handicapped children in Finland indicated that 4/61 or 6.6 per cent of boys and 2/50 or 4 per cent of girls had the fragile X (Kähkönen *et al.* 1987), while in the UK 14/156 (8.9 per cent) of boys with idiopathic severe mental retardation were fragile X positive (Bundey *et al.* 1985).

When Turner *et al.* (1980*b*) studied 72 phenotypically normal girls attending a school for the mildly mentally handicapped, they found 7 per cent of them to be carriers of the fragile X. Still in Australia, Sutherland (1985) performed studies on three handicapped populations, namely patients referred for chromosome studies, children attending special schools, and adults attending sheltered workshops. In the special schools 11/328 (3.35 per cent) boys and 2/174 (1.2 per cent) girls carried the marker X, whereas in the sheltered workshops the numbers were 0/84 and 0/44 respectively.

In Oklahoma, a survey of mentally handicapped males included both institutionalized and non-institutionalized schoolboys. Of the 65 subjects investigated, six (9.2 per cent) were found to have the fragile X syndrome (Carpenter *et al.* 1982). Across in Hawaii, Proops *et al.* (1983), studying 81 retarded school-aged children, found four (5 per cent) of them to have the marker X, while Rhoads (1984) found 2 per cent of males with mental retardation to be fragile X positive but 54 boys and 27 girls receiving special education were all negative, as were 107 patients attending a child-development clinic. In Hawaii, again, Jacobs *et al.* (1986) studied three further populations of retarded subjects. Among adults, on community placement, with IQ < 50 1.8 per cent of males and 0.4 per cent of females were marker X positive, among adults needing day-care facilities, 2.8 per cent of the men but no women were positive, and among children in school classes for the educationally subnormal 1.4 per cent of boys but no girls had the marker X chromosome.

A study in Southampton, UK, found no fragile X positive children among 166 attending schools for the moderately retarded (Lamont *et al.* 1986).

There have also been studies aimed at determining whether the marker X is present in normal populations. Kähkönen *et al.* (1987) found no evidence of the marker in a control group of 85 children; Abuelo *et al.* (1985) studied 36 normal adult females while Soudek and Gorzny (1980) studied 40 normal adult males, both studies reported negative findings and concluded that the fragile X was not present to a significant degree in normal populations. Sutherland (1982) obtained data on 1019 unselected newborns but did not detect any cases of fragile X. More recently, this series has been extended to include 3458 unselected neonates (1810 boys and 1648 girls) but again no marker X was detected (Sutherland 1985).

In two series of 'referred' patients where cultures were examined for the fragile X, Sutherland (1985) reported 13/2283 (0.526 per cent) of males and 3/1890 (0.15 per cent) of females as having the fragile X, where about one-half of the patients were retarded; while of a series of paediatric referrals in Italy, 5/2764 (0.18 per cent) boys and 2/2860 (0.07 per cent) girls were marker X positive. In this group, however, far fewer of the patients were referred for mental handicap (Groupo Siciliano di cooperazione per lo studio del cromosome X 1987).

Families

As there are several types of XLMR, families have been studied in order to establish the frequency with which the fragile X syndrome is segregating within them.

Jennings *et al.* (1980) found that 1/3 families with XLMR had the marker X, Turner *et al.* (1980*a*) found 1/3, Herbst *et al.* (1981) found 3/6, Mattei *et al.* (1981) found 3/6, and Proops *et al.* (1983) 1/3. In their study of seven families, however, Jacobs *et al.* (1980) reported that 6/7 had the marker.

When the number of XLMR families included those with affected females (as occurs in the fragile X syndrome) Bundey *et al.* (1985) found 5/13 to segregate the marker X, while Ishikiriyama and Niikawa (1983) found the marker in 2/21 families with two or more mentally retarded children.

Considering all these studies together it seems likely that approximately one-third of XLMR occurrence is due to the presence of the fragile X syndrome.

Individuals with macro-orchidism

While the correlation between mental retardation, macro-orchidism, and the fragile X syndrome is far from absolute, particularly among prepubertal boys (Cantu *et al.* 1976; Mattei *et al.* 1981), it is sufficiently strong for the presence of megalotestes to be used as a preliminary screening test in the selection of retarded males for cytogenetic studies aimed at the detection of the fragile X syndrome.

The first report of a family with XLMR and macro-orchidism (Escalante *et al.* 1971) was followed by several others (Turner *et al.* 1975; Bowen *et al.* 1978; Cantu *et al.* 1978). Later studies showed that the type of macro-orchidism involved was associated with the fragile X syndrome (Sutherland and Ashforth 1979; Turner *et al.* 1979; Carpenter *et al.* 1980; Martin *et al.* 1980; Sutherland *et al.* 1980; Vianna-Morgante *et al.* 1982), and it was suggested that they could be different manifestations of the same syndrome. As further pedigrees became available, however, it became evident that although macro-orchidism is a fairly good indicator for the fragile X syndrome, the correlation is by no means complete (Jacobs *et al.* 1979; Jennings *et al.* 1980; Mattei *et al.* 1981; Brøndum-Nielsen *et al.* 1982). Nevertheless, macro-orchidism has been used for the ascertainment of individuals who may have the marker X (Howard-Peebles and Stoddard 1979), and the measurement of testicular volume has been suggested as a screening procedure. Brown *et al.* (1981) selected 15 randomized adult males with non-specific mental retardation, measured their testes and found five to have a volume > 25 ml (above the 90th centile). Of these 4/5 had the fragile X. Other studies did not confirm this level of accuracy as a screening procedure. Howard-Peebles and Finley (1983) found only 7/17 White, mentally retarded men with very marked macro-orchidism (> 34 ml) to have the fragile X, while Kirklionis *et al.* (1983) found the marker X in only 11 per cent of their institutionalized males with testicular volume >25 ml. Shapiro *et al.* (1983), using a testicular volume of 25 ml as their cut-off point, found 10/23 or 44 per cent of their institutionalized males with macro-orchidism to have the fragile X syndrome, and suggested that testicular size could be used in conjunction with other clinical criteria for screening and detection of the syndrome.

Autistic populations

The relationship between autism and the fragile X is not yet fully understood. Since the early 1980s there have been many documented cases of autism associated with the fragile X (Turner *et al.* 1980*b*; Brown *et al.* 1982). In one of several Swedish studies Gillberg and Wahlström (1975), reporting on 66 cases of infantile autism, found a correlation, as 8/65 (25 per cent) had the marker. Gillberg's group (1987) also found that 4/20 (20 per cent) of children with Kanner-type autism also had the fragile X. Blomquist *et al.* (1985) found that out of 102 cases of infantile autism 13/83 (16 per cent) boys had the marker X but that none of the 19 girls did. When this study was extended to include 101 boys and 21 girls then 16 of the boys were found to have the fragile X, but still none of the girls did (Wahlstrom *et al.* 1986).

A lower frequency of the marker X in autistic males was reported by Watson *et al.* (1984) who found only 4/76 (5.3 per cent) of subjects to be fragile X positive. These authors also pointed out that this frequency is similar to that found in subjects with severe mental retardation.

In contrast, Venter *et al.* (1984) studied 40 boys and 17 girls who were autistic and unselected for family history, and found not a single fragile X positive case.

A different approach was taken by Levitas *et al.* (1983) who, instead of searching for the marker X in autistic children, looked for autism in patients with the fragile X syndrome. They found that of 10 patients with fragile X no less than six were also autistic.

A large multicentre survey of autistic children in the USA found 24/183 (13.1 per cent) of males to be positive for the fragile X, and, conversely, that 17.3 per cent of fragile X males were also autistic (Brown *et al.* 1986). Hagerman *et al.* (1986*a*) raised the question of diagnosis of autism in males with the marker, as they found that while 16 per cent of 50 fragile X positive males fulfilled all the criteria for the diagnosis of infantile autism, some traits were present in almost all of them. These authors also reported an association between autism and the fragile X syndrome in two mentally retarded women (Hagerman *et al.* 1986*b*).

Institutionalized populations

Surveys of institutionalized populations have been carried out in various parts of the world, and while they do provide a measure of the contribution of the fragile X syndrome to morbidity, they should be used with caution in epidemiological studies. They cannot be employed to provide estimates of prevalence as the populations are not only undefined but also reflect the policy of institutionalization of mentally handicapped people within that society.

Among studies performed in Europe, Froster-Iskenius *et al.* (1983) found 15/242 (6.2 per cent) of males with severe mental retardation to have the fragile X, while Kähkönen *et al.* (1983) reported 6/150 (4 per cent). However, when a subgroup of these patients with no dysmorphic features, neurological signs, or childhod psychoses was considered, this figure rose to 8.8 per cent. Similar findings were observed in Italy where, of 349 institutionalized individuals, 7.7 per cent of the males and 4.1 per cent of the females were marker X positive (*Gruppo Siciliano di cooperazione per studio del cromosa X* 1987).

In the UK, English (1986) found 29/365 (7.9 per cent) of males within one institution to carry the fragile X chromosome, while Primrose *et al.* (1986) detected two severely retarded marker X positive females among 20 families with a history of mental retardation. In 1972, Turner *et al.* had suggested that XLMR without physical signs accounted for the male preponderance in institutions for the mentally retarded. In 1982, Sutherland investigated three such institutions in the course of his population studies and found 7/444 (1.6 per cent) of males but 0/80 females to be marker X positive.

In the USA, a study of institutionalized individuals in Massachusetts (Paika *et al.* 1984) revealed 6/144 (4.1 per cent) of males with idiopathic mental retardation to be fragile X positive, and a study from Colorado (Jackson, personal communication) demonstrated the marker X in 8/143 (5.6 per cent) males and 1/57 females.

Two studies from Hawaii, the first on 274 retarded males (Jacobs *et al.* 1983) and the second on 278 retarded females (Mayer *et al.* 1985), detected only 5 (1.8 per cent) of the males and one (0.4 per cent) of the females as marker X positive. All of these subjects were, however, on community placement from an institution and so may not have been comparable to those in other studies.

Similar surveys carried out in Japan reported that of 243 institutionalized males, 13 (5.3 per cent) had fragile X, but if only those males with mental retardation of unknown aetiology were considered, then this percentage rose to 8.6 per cent (Arinami *et al.* 1986). Of 190 institutionalized Japanese females, the only two with fragile X were both severely retarded (3.3 per cent of severely retarded females with no known cause), whereas of 35 moderately retarded females none had the marker (Arinami *et al.* 1987).

When comparing this type of study (Table 2.3) it must be remembered that some authors include all the subjects within an institution in their populations while others consider only those subjects with mental retardation of unknown aetiology.

Different nationalities

The fragile X syndrome has been detected in every ethnic group in which it has been sought. Although XLMR was once believed to be most prevalent in families of North European origin (Herbst 1980), later work has shown that this is most probably due to ascertainment bias.

Individual reports soon caused the fragile X syndrome to be identified in southern European communities, e.g. Spanish (Kaiser-McKaw *et al.* 1980; Lopez-Pajares *et al.* 1983; Sordo *et al.* 1983), Italian (Sanfillippo *et al.* 1986), and Greek (Mavrou *et al.* 1987).

The first report of the fragile X in an individual of non-European extraction came from Howard-Peebles and Stoddard (1980) who detected the marker X in a Black American family, as did Carpenter *et al.* in 1982.

Mattei *et al.* (1981) reported on families of North African origin; in Central and South America, families with the fragile X syndrome were ascertained in Mexico (Rivera *et al.* 1981), Brazil (Vianna-Morgante *et al.* 1982), and Chile (Lacassie *et al.* 1982); while from the Indian subcontinent came a report of a Sri-Lankan family (Soysa *et al.* 1982) and a family of Indian origin resident in South Africa (Gardner *et al.* 1983). Two boys from Pakistani families were detected in a study from the UK (Bundey *et al.* 1985).

The Orient is represented by reports of the detection of the marker X in Japan (Ishikiriyama and Niikawa 1983, Arinami *et al.* 1986, 1987) and among some residents of Hawaii (Rhoads *et al.* 1982).

The undertaking of larger studies meant that in communities of mixed ethnic origin the fragile X could be observed in several nationalities within one study. Bundey *et al.* (1985) reported the finding of fragile X positive individuals from both Asian and European communities in the UK, while Rhoads (1984) ascertained nine Hawaiian families of whom two were of Japanese origin, three Caucasian, one Japanese–Caucasian, one Filipino–Caucasian, one Dutch–Indonesian, and one part-Hawaiian. Jacobs *et al.* (1986), reporting on the distribution of the marker X syndrome within the racial groups of Hawaii, found no significant differences in the prevalance of the syndrome in Caucasian, Hawaiian, Oriental, or Filipino families.

Table 2.3. The detection of fragile Xq27 in institutionalized populations

Study	Location	Number of males studied	% Incidence of fragile X syndrome	Number of females studied	% Incidence of fragile X syndrome
Froster-Iskenius *et al.* (1983)	Germany	242	6.2		
Kähkönen *et al.* (1983)	Finland	150	4.0 (8.8)		
English (1986)	UK	365	7.9		
Sutherland (1985)	Australia	444	1.6		
Paika *et al.* (1984)	USA	144	4.1		
Jacobs *et al.* (1983)	Hawaii	274	1.8		
Mayer *et al.* (1985)	Hawaii			278	0.4
Arinami *et al.* (1986, 1987)	Japan	243	5.3 (8.6)	190	3.3
Gruppo Siciliano di cooperazione per lo studio del cromosoma X (1987)	Italy	155	7.7	194	4.1

The figures in brackets refer to the percentage of fragile X positive individuals obtained when a more stringent selection procedure is applied to the same population (see text).

Similar studies were carried out in South Africa by Venter *et al.* (1981, 1982). In a study of non-specific mental retardation in males, these authors ascertained nine families with the fragile X syndrome, including Black (Zulu), Cape-coloured, Indian, and White.

References

Abuelo, D., Castree, K., Pueschel, S., Padre-Mendoza, T., and Zolnierez, K. (1985). Frequency of fragile X chromosome in normal females. *Clinical Genetics*, **28**, 97–9.

Arinami, T., Kundo, I., and Nakajima, S. (1986). Frequency of the fragile X syndrome in Japanese mentally retarded males. *Human Genetics*, **73**, 309–12.

Arinami, T., Kundo, I., Nakajima, S., and Hamaguchi, H. (1987). Frequency of the fragile X syndrome in institutionalized mentally retarded females in Japan. *Human Genetics*, **76**, 344–7.

Blomquist, H. K., Gustavson, K. H., and Holmgren, G. (1981). Mild mental retardation in children in a Northern Swedish county. A prevalance study. *Journal of Mental Deficiency Research*, **25**, 169–86.

Blomquist, H. K., Gustavson, K. H., Holmgren, G., Nordenson, I., and Sweins, A. (1982). Fragile X chromosomes and X-linked mental retardation in severely retarded boys in a Northern Swedish county. A prevalence study. *Clinical Genetics*, **21**, 209–14.

Blomquist, H. K., Gustavson, K. H., Holmgren, G., Nordenson, I., and Palsson-Strae, U. (1983). Fragile X syndrome in mildly mentally retarded children in a Northern Swedish county. A prevalence study. *Clinical Genetics*, **24**, 393–8.

Blomquist, H. K. *et al.* (1985). Frequency of the fragile X syndrome in infantile autism. A swedish multicenter study. *Clinical Genetics*, **27**, 113–17.

Bowen, P., Biederman, B., and Swallow, K. A. (1978). The X-linked syndrome of macro-orchidism and mental retardation: further observations. *American Journal of Medical Genetics*, **2**, 409–14.

Brøndum-Nielsen, K., Tommerup, N., Dyggve, H. V., and Schou, C. (1982). Macro-orchidism and fragile X in mentally retarded males. *Human Genetics*, **61**, 113–17.

Brown, W. T., Mezzacarpa, P. M., and Jenkins, E. C. (1981). Screening for fragile X syndrome by testicular size measurement. *Lancet*, **ii**, 1055.

Brown, W. T. *et al.* (1982). Association of fragile-X syndrome with autism. *Lancet*, **i**, 100.

Brown, W. T. *et al.* (1986). Fragile X and autism: a multicenter survey. *American Journal of Medical Genetics*, **23**, 341–53.

Bundey, S., Webb, T., Thake, A., and Todd, J. (1985). A community study of severe mental retardation in the West Midlands and the importance of the fragile X chromosome in its aetiology. *Journal of Medical Genetics*, **22**, 258–66.

Cantu, J. M. *et al.* (1976). Inherited congenital normo-functional testicular hyperplasia and mental deficiency. *Human Genetics*, **33**, 23–33.

Cantu, J. M. *et al.* (1978). Inherited congenital normo-functional testicular hyperplasia and mental deficiency. *Human Genetics*, **41**, 331–9.

Carpenter, N. J., Leichtman, L. G., Munshi, G., Fullerton, P. S., and Say, B. (1980). The marker X chromosome among families with and without histories of X-linked mental retardation. *American Journal of Human Genetics*, **32**, 65A.

Carpenter, N. J., Leichtman, L. G., and Say, B. (1982). Fragile X-linked mental retardation. A survey of 65 patients with mental retardation of unknown origin. *American Journal of Diseases of Children*, **136**, 392–8.

English, C. (1986). Unpublished Ph.D. thesis. Cytogenetic, anthropometric and inheritance studies in the fragile X syndrome. University of Newcastle-Upon-Tyne.

Escalanté, J. A., Grunspun, H., and Frota-Pessoa, O. (1971). Severe sex-linked mental retardation. *Journal de Génétique Humaine*, **19**, 137–40.

Fishburn, J., Turner, G., Daniel, A., and Brookwell, R. (1983). The diagnosis and frequency of X-linked conditions in a cohort of moderately retarded males with affected brothers. *American Journal of Medical Genetics*, **14**, 713–24.

Froster-Iskenius, U., Felsch, G., Schirren, C., and Schwinger, E. (1983). Screening for fra(X)(q) in a population of mentally retarded males. *Human Genetics*, **63**, 153–7.

Gardner, R. J. M., Smart, R. D., Cornell, J. M., Merckel, L. M., and Beighton, P. (1983). The fragile X chromosome in a large Indian kindred. *Clinical Genetics*, **23**, 311–17.

Gillberg, C., and Wahlstrom, J. (1975). Chromosome abnormalities in infantile autism and other childhood psychoses. A population study of 66 cases. *Developmental Medicine and Child Neurology*, **29**, 641–9.

Gillberg, C., Steffenburg, S., and Jakobsson, G. (1987). Neurobiological findings in 20 relatively gifted children with Kanner-type autism or Asperger syndrome. *Developmental Medicine and Child Neurology*, **29**, 641–9.

Gruppo Siciliano di cooperazione per lo studio del cromosoma X fragile (1987). *The fragile X in Sicily: an epidemiological survey.* Third International Workshop on the Fragile X and X-linked Mental Retardation. Troina, 13–16 September.

Gustavson, K. H., Holmgren, G., Jonsell, R., and Blomquist, H. K. (1977). Severe mental retardation in children in a Northern Swedish county. *Journal of Mental Deficiency Research*, **21**, 161–80.

Gustavson, K. H., Blomquist, H. K., and Holmgren, G. (1986). Prevalence of the fragile-X syndrome in mentally retarded children in a Swedish county. *American Journal of Medical Genetics*, **23**, 581–7.

Hagerman, R. J., Jackson, A. W., Levitas, A., Rimland, B., and Braden, M. (1986*a*). An analysis of autism in fifty males with the fragile X syndrome. *American Journal of Medical Genetics*, **23**, 359–75.

Hagerman, R. J., Chudley, A. E., Knoll, J. H., Jackson, A. W., Kemper, M., and Ahmad, R. (1986*b*). Autism in fragile-X females. *American Journal of Medical Genetics*, **23**, 375–81.

Herbst, D. S. (1980). Non-specific X-linked mental retardation 1: A review with information from 24 new families. *American Journal of Medical Genetics*, **7**, 443–60.

Herbst, D. S. and Miller, J. R. (1980). Nonspecific X-linked mental retardation 11: The frequency in British Columbia. *American Journal of Medical Genetics*, **7**, 461–9.

Herbst, D. S., Dunn, H. G., Dill, F. J., Kalousek, D. K., and Krywaniuk, L. W. (1981). Further delineation of X-linked mental retardation. *Human Genetics*, **58**, 366–72.

Howard-Peebles, P. N. (1982). Non-specific mental retardation: background, types, diagnosis and prevalence. *Journal of Mental Deficiency Research*, **26**, 205–13.

Howard-Peebles, P. N. and Finley, W. H. (1983). Screening of mentally retarded males for macro-orchidism and the fragile X chromosome. *American Journal of Medical Genetics*, **15**, 631–5.

Howard-Peebles, P. N. and Stoddard, G. R. (1979). X-linked mental retardation with macro-orchidism and marker X chromosomes. *Human Genetics*, **50**, 247–51.

Howard-Peebles, P. N. and Stoddard, G. R. (1980). Race distribution in X-linked mental retardation with macro-orchidism and fragile site in Xq. *American Journal of Human Genetics*, **32**, 629–30.

Ishikiriyama, S. and Niikawa, N. (1983). Two Japanese patients with fragile X syndrome. *Teratology*, **28**, 30A.

Jacobs, P. A. *et al.* (1979). More on marker X chromosome and mental retardation and macro-orchidism. *New England Journal of Medicine*, **300**, 737–8.

Jacobs, P. A. *et al.* (1980). X-linked mental retardation: a study of 7 families. *American Journal of Medical Genetics*, **7**, 471–89.

Jacobs, P. A., Mayer, M., Matsuura, J., Rhoads, F., and Yee, S. C. (1983). a cytogenetic study of a population of mentally retarded males with special reference to the marker(X) syndrome. *Human Genetics*, **7**, 471–89.

Jacobs, P., Mayer, M., and Abruzzo, M. A. (1986). Studies of the fragile(X) syndrome in populations of mentally retarded individuals in Hawaii. *American Journal of Medical Genetics*, **23**, 567–72.

Jennings, M., Hall, J. G., and Hoehn, H. (1980). Significance of phenotypic and chromosomal abnormalities in X-linked mental retardation (Martin–Bell or Renpenning syndrome). *American Journal of Medical Genetics*, **7**, 417–32.

Kähkönen, M., Leisti, J., Wilska, M., and Varonen, S. (1983). Marker X associated mental retardation. A study of 150 retarded males. *Clinical Genetics*, **23**, 397–404.

Kähkönen, M. *et al.* (1987). Prevalence of the fragile X syndrome in four birth cohorts of children of school age. *Human Genetics*, **77**, 85–7.

Kaiser-McKaw, B., Hecht, F., Cadien, J. D., and Moore, B. C. (1980). Fragile X linked mental retardation. *American Journal of Medical Genetics*, **7**, 503–5.

Kirkilionis, A., Sergovich, F., and Pozsonyi, J. (1983). Use of testicular volume as a cytogenetic screening criterion. *American Journal of Human Genetics*, **35**, 138A.

Lacassie, Y. S. *et al.* (1982). The fragile X syndrome. Report of the first patients cytogenetically confirmed in Chile. *Revista Chilena de Pediatria*, **54**, 410–16.

Lamont, M. A., Dennis, N. R., and Seabright, M. (1986). Chromosome abnormalities in pupils attending ESN/M schools. *Archives of Diseases in Childhood*, **61**, 223–6.

Levitas, A., Hagerman, R. J., Braden, M., Rimland, B., McBogg, P., and Matus, I. (1983). Autism and the fragile-X syndrome. *Journal of Developmental and Behavioural Pediatrics*, **4**, 151–8.

Lopez-Pajares, I., Delicado, A., Gallego, A., and Pascual-Castroviejo, I. (1983). Familial X-linked retardation and fragile X chromosomes in 6 Spanish families. *Clinical Genetics*, **23**, 236.

Martin, R. H., Lin, C. C., Mathies, B. J., and Lowry, R. B. (1980). X-linked mental retardation with macro-orchidism and marker-X chromosomes. *American Journal of Medical Genetics*, **7**, 433–41.

Mattei, J. F., Mattei, M. G., Aumeras, C., Auger, M., and Giraud, F. (1981). X-linked mental retardation with the fragile X. A study of 15 families. *Human Genetics*, **59**, 281–9.

Mavrou, A., Syrrou, M., Tsenghi, C., Agelakis, Y., Ouroukos, S., and Metaxotou, C. (1987). Fragile X syndrome and mental retardation in Greece. Third International Workshop on the Fragile X and X-linked Mental Retardation. Troina, September 13–16.

Mayer, M., Abruzzo, M. A., Jacobs, P. A., and Yee, S. C. (1985). A cytogenetic study of a population of retarded females with special reference to the fragile (X) syndrome. *Human Genetics*, **69**, 206–8.

Paika, I. J., Lai, F., McAllister, N. M., and Miller, W. A. (1984). The fragile-X marker survey: preliminary report on the screening of suspected fragile-X syndrome patients at Fernald State School. *American Journal of Human Genetics*, **36**, 108S.

Priest, J. H., Thuline, H. C., La Veck, G. B., and Jarvis, D. B. (1961). An approach to genetic factors in mental retardation. *American Journal of Mental Deficiency*, **66**, 42–50.

Primrose, D. A., El Matmati, R., Boyd, E., Gosden, C., and Newton, M. (1986). Prevalence of the fragile-X syndrome in an institution for the mentally handicapped. *British Journal of Psychiatry*, **148**, 655–7.

Proops, R., Mayer, M., and Jacobs, P. A. (1983). a study of mental retardation in children on the island of Hawaii. *Clinical Genetics*, **23**, 81–96.

Rhoads, F. A. (1984). Fragile-X syndrome in Hawaii: a summary of clinical experience. *American Journal of Medical Genetics*, **17**, 209–14.

Rhoads, F. A., Oglesby, A. C., Mayer, M., and Jacobs, P. A. (1982). Marker X syndrome in an oriental family with probable transmission by a normal male. *American Journal of Medical Genetics*, **12**, 205–17.

Rivera, H., Hernandez, A., Plascencia, L., Sanchez-Corona, J., Garcia-Cruz, D., and Cantu, J. M. (1981). Some observations on the mental deficiency, normo-functional testicular hyperplasia and fra(X)(q28) chromosome syndrome. *Annales de Génétique*, **24**, 220–2.

Sanfillippo, S., Ragusa, R. M., Musumeci, S., and Neri, G. (1986). Fragile X mental retardation: Prevalence in a group of institutionalised patients in Italy and description of a novel EEG pattern. *American Journal of Medical Genetics*,

23, 589–95.

Shapiro, L. R., Summa, G. M., Wilmot, P. L., and Gloth, E. (1983). Screening and detection of the fragile X syndrome. *American Journal of Human Genetics*, **35**, 117A.

Sherman, S. L., Morton, N. E., Jacobs, P. A., and Turner, G. (1984). The marker(X) syndrome: a cytogenetic and genetic analysis. *Annals of Human Genetics*, **48**, 21–37.

Sordo, M. T., Estevez de Pablo, C., Guzman, M., Quintana-Castilla, A., and san Roman, C. (1983). Familial X-linked mental retardation. *Clinical Genetics*, **23**, 247.

Soudek, D. and Gorzny, N. (1980). No fragile X chromosome in normal men. *Clinical Genetics*, **19**, 140–1.

Soysa, P., Senanayahe, M., Mikkelsen, M., and Poulsen, H. (1982). Martin–Bell syndrome fra(X)(q28) in a Sri-Lankan family. *Journal of Mental Deficiency Research*, **26**, 251–7.

Sutherland, G. R. (1982). Heritable fragile sites on human chromosomes VIII. Preliminary population cytogenetic data on the folic-acid-sensitive fragile sites. *American Journal of Human Genetics*, **34**, 452–8.

Sutherland, G. R. (1985). Heritable fragile sites on human chromosomes XII. Population cytogenetics. *Annals of Human Genetics*, **49**, 153–61.

Sutherland, G. R. and Ashforth, P. L. C. (1979). X-linked mental retardation with macro-orchidism and fragile site at Xq27. *Human Genetics*, **48**, 117–20.

Sutherland, G. R., Judge, C. G., and Wiener, S. (1980). Familial X-linked mental retardation with an X chromosome abnormality and macro-orchidism. *Journal of Medical Genetics*, **17**, 73.

Turner, G. and Jacobs, P. (1983). Marker (X)-linked mental retardation. *Advances in Human Genetics*, **13**, 83–112.

Turner, G. and Turner, B. (1974). X-linked mental retardation. *Journal of Medical Genetics*, **11**, 109–13.

Turner, G., Turner, B., and Collins, E. (1970). Renpennings syndrome X-linked mental retardation. *Lancet*, **ii**, 365–6.

Turner, G., Engisch, B., Lindsay, D. G., and Turner, B. (1972). X-linked mental retardation without physical abnormality (Renpennings syndrome) in sibs in an institution. *Journal of Medical Genetics*, **9**, 324–30.

Turner, G., Eastman, C., Casey, J., McLeay, A., Procopis, P., and Turner, B. (1975). X-linked mental retardation associated with macro-orchidism. *Journal of Medical Genetics*, **12**, 367–71.

Turner, G., Gill, R., and Daniel, A. (1979). Marker X chromosome mental retardation and macro-orchidism. *New England Journal of Medicine*, **299**, 1472.

Turner, G., Brookwell, R., Daniel, A., Selikowitz, M., and Zilibowitz, M. (1980*a*). Heterozygous expression of X-linked mental retardation and X-chromosome marker fra(X)(q27). *New England Journal of Medicine*, **303**, 662–4.

Turner, G., Daniel, A., and Frost, M. (1980*b*). X-linked mental retardation, macro-orchidism and the Xq27 fragile site. *Journal of Pediatrics*, **96**, 836–41.

Turner, G., Robinson, H., Laing, S., and Purvis-Smith, S. (1986). Preventative screening for the fragile-X syndrome. *New England Journal of Medicine*, **315**, 607–9.

Venter, P. A. and Op't Hof, J. (1982). Cytogenetic abnormalities including the marker-X chromsome in patients with severe mental retardation. *South African Medical Journal*, **62**, 947.

Venter, P. A., Gericke, G. S., Dawson, B., and Op't Hof, J. (1981). A marker X chromosome associated with non-specific male mental retardation. *South African Medical Journal*, **60**, 807–11.

Venter, P. A., Op't Hof, J., Coetzee, D. J., and Van de Welt Retaf, A. E. (1984). No marker X in autistic children. *Human Genetics*, **67**, 107.

Vianna-Morgante, A. M., Armando, I., and Frota-Pessoa, O. (1982). Escalante syndrome and the marker X chromosome. *American Journal of Medical Genetics*, **12**, 237–40.

Wahlstrom, J., Gillberg, C., Gustavson, K. H., and Holmgren, G. (1986). Infantile autism and the fragile-X. A Swedish multicentre study. *American Journal of Medical Genetics*, **23**, 403–8.

Watson, M. S. *et al.* (1984). Fragile-X in a survey of 75 autistic males. *New England Journal of Medicine*, **310**, 1462.

Webb, T., Bundey, S., Thake, J., and Todd, A. (1986). The frequency of the fragile X chromosome among schoolchildren in Coventry. *Journal of Medical Genetics*, **23**, 396–9.

3 Behaviour and treatment of the fragile X syndrome

RANDI HAGERMAN

Introduction

The behaviour of fragile X males is characteristic of the syndrome and perhaps more helpful diagnostically than the physical features. This is most important in young fragile X boys because usually they do not manifest a long, narrow face or macro-orchidism. The clinician must be alert to the behavioural manifestations in fragile X boys so that the diagnostic chromosomal analysis for fragile X will be considered. Although a fragile X boy may present with a range of problems from language delay to autism, there is a similarity in all of the affected males. Perhaps it is the combination of attentional difficulties with unusual features such as hand mannerisms, poor eye contact, and limited cognitive abilities that begins to clue the clinician into this specific diagnosis. It would be easier to demonstrate the diagnosis by videotape because there are similarities in movement, particularly the approach to and withdrawal from people, hand mannerisms, and speech that are difficult to describe in words. There is also significant variation from individual to individual. However, the similarities in behaviour will be stressed in this chapter so that a better understanding of the impact of the fragile X gene on brain function can be gained. The behaviour of fragile X males is a feature of how their brains are organized, including cognitive, language, and sensory motor integration abilities. All of these aspects will be reviewed along with notable behavioural characteristics of fragile X males and females.

Cognitive features

There is a broad spectrum of cognitive involvement in the fragile X syndrome. In males, the degree of retardation ranges from profound to mild, but higher functioning males also exist. They are affected by the syndrome and are fragile X positive but they have an IQ in the borderline or low normal range (Sherman *et al.* 1984; Hagerman *et al.* 1985; Goldfine *et al.* 1987; Theobald *et al.* 1987; Veenema *et al.* 1987). They are clearly different from the non-penetrant, transmitting males who are unaffected by the syndrome and represent approximately 20 per cent of males who carry the fragile X gene (Sherman *et al.* 1984, 1985; Howard-Peebles and Friedman 1985; Froster-Iskenius *et al.* 1986*a*). An occasional male has been reported as fragile X positive but apparently 'normal', although detailed psychological testing of these males has not been reported (Daker *et al.* 1981; Webb *et al.* 1986). They may be non-penetrant males, although these males are usually considered fragile X negative and without any cognitive deficits or behavioural problems. Loesch *et al.* (1987) have performed limited cognitive testing of presumably 'non-penetrant' males and found that some are fragile X positive and learning disabled or behaviourally disturbed. Perhaps some so-called 'non-penetrant' males are really mildly penetrant for a limited number of behavioural and/or cognitive features of the fragile X syndrome. More detailed psychological testing is necessary in a larger number of 'non-penetrant' males.

The majority of adult fragile X males function cognitively in the moderately to severely retarded range (Opitz and Sutherland 1984). Their language and non-language skills are relatively similar (Newell *et al.* 1983) although isolated areas of language, such as single-word vocabulary, may be significantly higher than isolated non-verbal tasks, such as spatial reasoning (Theobald *et al.* 1987). This is a reflection of the learning strengths and weaknesses, or cognitive profiles, which are relatively consistent in the fragile X syndrome. On the Stanford–Binet assessment, Kemper *et al.* (1988) have noted rather consistent patterns, including difficulties with number concepts and consistent strengths in vocabulary and other areas of verbal facility. This pattern has also been seen in four higher-functioning fragile X boys (Hagerman *et al.* 1985) who demonstrated marked difficulties in arithmetic and relative strengths in early reading and vocabulary skills. These higher-functioning fragile X males also demonstrated a higher Simultaneous Processing IQ than Sequential Processing IQ on the Kaufman Assessment Battery for Children. Kemper *et al.* (1988) has confirmed this finding in a controlled study, and Leckman *et al.* (1987) has documented this finding in both children and adult fragile X males. The presence of a specific cognitive profile has important implications in the creation of educational programmes for fragile X boys, as discussed in a later section of this chapter.

There is evidence to suggest that a significant decline in IQ scores will occur in fragile X males throughout childhood. Several investigators have documented this trend retrospectively (Herbst *et al.* 1981; Chudley *et al.* 1983; Hagerman *et al.* 1983; Partington 1984). In early childhood fragile X boys often present as mildly retarded, but when identified as adults they are often moderately or severely retarded. These studies may have been biased by the preponderance of adults found in institutional settings. Lachiewicz *et al.* (1987) recently presented a retrospective study of IQ changes over time in 21 fragile X boys who were not institutionalized. The group as a whole demonstrated a significant IQ drop, with 13 boys individually showing a significant decline. This trend was also seen in a longitudinal study of 10 fragile X boys recently presented by Leckman *et al.* (1987). All of the boys demonstrated a significant IQ decline after 10 years of age. Our experience (Hagerman *et al.* 1987*b*) includes an analysis of 18 non-institutionalized fragile X boys who were followed for a mean of six years through childhood. There was a mean drop in IQ of 6.9 points for the group; however, individual analysis demonstrated a significant IQ drop in only five patients. As the child ages, a greater emphasis is placed on abstract thinking ability which is a significant area of deficit for all fragile X males. Intellectual deterioration or a loss of milestones does not occur in fragile X. However, a decrease in the IQ score which can be seen in a significant number of males appears to be related to the increasing demands on abstract thinking and the increasingly complex problem-solving skills required of older children. This trend may not be dissimilar to other groups of retarded individuals (Fisher and Zeaman 1970).

Speech

Fragile X males usually present in early childhood with both speech and language delays. Single words may not be uttered until after 2 years of age and phrases and short sentences are delayed until 3 years of age or older. A limited number of fragile X males may be completely non-verbal and these individuals are usually severely or profoundly retarded and often institutionalized as adults. The majority of males have a rather characteristic speech pattern that many early reports of fragile X patients described as jocular, litany, or staccato speech (Howard-Peebles *et al.* 1979; Jacobs *et al.* 1980; Turner *et al.* 1980; Herbst *et al.* 1981). In a detailed analysis of 21 fragile X males, Newell *et al.* (1983) described a variety of deficits in both the receptive and expressive areas, including dysfluencies, perseverations, echolalia, palilalia (reiteration of the speaker's own words and phrases in a perseverative manner), and auditory processing and memory deficits. Paul *et al.* (1984) also documented dysfluency and dyspraxia in three fragile X boys. In evaluating higher-functioning fragile X boys, Hanson *et al.* (1986) described cluttering, a fast and fluctuating rate of speech, which includes dysfluencies, poor topic maintenance, and, occasionally, garbled speech. Largo and Schinzel (1985) have described frequent articulation problems with delayed symbolic play in the majority of 17 fragile X boys. Madison *et al.* (1986*a*) described hypernasal speech but found that grammar was appropriate for mental age in five males, and this was also noted by Newell *et al.* (1983) in 17 males. Although these studies are descriptive, none are controlled to evaluate whether the many unusual characteristics of fragile X speech are intrinsic to the syndrome or related only to the level of retardation.

Wolf-Schein *et al.* (1987) compared 35 fragile X males to 15 Down syndrome males matched for cognitive ability and found significant differences in their speech characteristics, using a standardized format. Down syndrome males demonstrated more referential gestures and non-verbal facial and head signals, whereas fragile X males demonstrated more stereotyped vocalizations, jargon, dysrhythmia, perseveration, echolalia, conditioned statements, inappropriate tangential comments, and more frequently talked to themselves. The unusual speech pattern of fragile X males is not simply a function of lowered cognitive ability. Further controlled studies comparing the speech of fragile X males to autistic non-fragile X males will be helpful in characterizing the truly unique aspects of fragile X speech.

Behaviour

The behaviour of fragile X boys usually includes hyperactivity with a short attention span, perseverative or cluttered speech, and often unusual hand mannerisms, such as hand-flapping or hand-biting. Many are friendly and enjoy the company of people, but features such as poor eye contact and tactile defensiveness interfere with social interactions. The juxtaposition of a friendly personality with some unusual autistic-like features has fuelled the controversy of autism in fragile X.

Autism

The coexistence of autism and the fragile X syndrome was first described by Brown *et al.* (1982) in five fragile X males who fulfilled the DSM III (APA 1980) criteria for autism. Subsequent reports have found a variable association and the incidence of autism in fragile X has ranged from 5 per cent to 53 per cent (Brown *et al.* 1986*a*). Most of the variability in these numbers relates to the fact that researchers have used different diagnostic criteria for defining autism. It is perhaps more appropriate and helpful to the clinician to delineate the specific features which are seen commonly in fragile X boys and are considered autistic features.

In a study of 50 unselected fragile X males (Hagerman *et al.* 1986*b*), the presence of several behaviours were documented by examination and history. Hand-flapping was seen in 66 per cent, hand-biting in 74 per cent, and poor eye contact in 90 per cent. Only 18 per cent demonstrated a pervasive lack of relatedness, and only 16 per cent fulfilled DSM III criteria for autism, although 30 per cent fulfilled the Autism Behavior Checklist Criteria for autism. Cohen *et al.* (1988) compared the behaviour of non-autistic fragile X males to non-autistic retarded males, normal controls, and non-fragile X autistic males. Stranger-avoidance occurred at higher rates in all fragile X subjects compared to non-fragile X autistics and the other control groups. This feature in fragile X patients was not related to the degree of retardation nor to the language level, which were both controlled for in the comparison groups. Instead, the poor eye contact was associated with the general social avoidance of both parents and strangers and appeared to be an intrinsic property of the fragile X diagnosis itself. Although most fragile X males are not autistic, the majority have some autistic-like features and fit the DSM III (APA 1980) diagnostic category of childhood onset Pervasive Developmental Disorder or Atypical Pervasive Developmental Disorder. The recognition of these behavioural difficulties are important not only for diagnosis, but also for treatment. These behavioural difficulties cause the family significant distress which necessitates intervention both at home and at school.

Hyperactivity

Hyperactivity is often the presenting problem in a fragile X child. It begins in early childhood and is associated with a short attention span. The child's attention often jumps from one area of interest to another within minutes or seconds and the child appears disorganized and impulsive. Attentional problems and hyperactivity were described by many researchers, including Mattei *et al.* (1981) in his description of 15 boys, Fryns *et al.* (1984) in 21 fragile X boys, and Finelli *et al.* (1985) who described hyperactivity in 47 per cent of 17 patients. Largo and Schinzel (1985) also described hyperactivity, beginning at 2 years of age, in 13 fragile X boys. Hyperactivity can also be the presenting feature in non-retarded fragile X boys (Hagerman *et al.* 1985). Seventy-three per cent of 37 prepubertal males followed in Denver fulfilled DSM III (APA 1980) criteria for Attention Deficit Disorder and had a Conners' Rating Scale score (Conners 1973) in the hyperactive range (Hagerman 1987).

All of the prepubertal fragile X males have some degree of attentional problems whether they are hyperactive or not. This is an important behavioural feature of fragile X because it can be treated, as discussed below.

Associated with the attentional problems are other perceptual, speech, and motor difficulties, similar to non-fragile X children with autism. Sensory inconstancies (Ornitz and Ritvo 1968) and difficulty in integrating sensory stimuli are probably the cause of the unusual behavioural characteristics in fragile X. Fragile X children are easily overwhelmed by excessive sensory stimuli, such as shopping malls or crowds, and they may react by an increase in repetitive behaviours or tantrums. The recent findings of a decrease in the size of the posterior vermis of the cerebellum, as seen by MRI scanning (Reiss and Patel 1987) in four fragile X males, supports the clinical observations of difficulty with sensory integration. The vermis of the cerebellum is a major locus for the co-ordination and integration of motor and sensory stimuli.

Heterozygous females

Approximately one-third of heterozygotes are considered cognitively impaired (Sherman *et al.* 1985; Fryns 1986) and this usually refers to IQ ability below 80. Chudley *et al.* (1983) reported an inverse correlation between IQ and percentage of lymphocytes which demonstrate the fragile X chromosome. However, approximately 40 per cent of heterozygotes are neither fragile X positive nor affected cognitively, and this has complicated carrier detection and genetic counselling. Kemper *et al.* (1986) has reported the presence of learning disabilities in normal-IQ heterozygotes; including deficits in maths, which appear to be a milder version of the deficits seen in fragile X males. A characteristic cognitive profile has also been noted in the learning-disabled heterozygous females, and this consists of lowered scores on Arithmetic, Digit Span, and Block Design of the WISC-R (Kemper *et al.* 1986; Miezejeski *et al.* 1986). Grigsby *et al.* (1987) has documented the presence of Gerstmann syndrome in several affected heterozygotes and a high-functioning fragile X boy. The Gerstmann syndrome includes dyscalculia, dysgraphia, right–left confusion, and finger agnosia, and is associated with lesions of the dominant parietal lobe. Although such lesions have never been documented in fragile X patients, the brain anatomy in fragile X requires further study.

Wolff *et al.* (1988) have performed neuropsychological evaluations of 15 non-retarded heterozygotes and matched controls. The heterozygotes as a group demonstrated lowered academic abilities than the controls, and arithmetic was the lowest achievement area. Fifty-three per cent of the heterozygotes were identified as learning-disabled. It appears that the spectrum of cognitive involvement in heterozygotes is broad, and affected females may have a normal IQ.

The subtle effects of the fragile X gene on neuro-cognitive functioning may also impact emotional development. Anecdotal reports of shy and socially withdrawn behaviour are common in the sisters of fragile X males. An occasional autistic heterozygote has been reported (Hagerman *et al.* 1986*c*; Edwards *et al.* 1987) and there appears to be a spectrum of social withdrawal that is milder than in the males. The behavioural features of young mildly affected heterozygotes can include frequent socially inappropriate comments, poor modulation of verbal tone, odd communication patterns, and tangential speech. Only rarely are stereotypes such as hand-biting or hand-flapping seen. Fryns (1986) reported psychiatric problems (psychotic behaviour was the most frequent problem) in 10 per cent of mentally normal heterozygotes and in 20 per cent of mentally subnormal heterozygotes. Although he studied 144 heterozygotes, his emphasis was on the physical and cognitive features and the details of the psychiatric evaluation were not reported.

Reiss *et al.* (1988*a*) have carried out a detailed psychiatric evaluation of 35 obligate carriers and 24 fragile X negative controls, and found that one-third of the heterozygotes met diagnostic criteria for schizotypal features, which included inadequate rapport due to constricted or inappropriate effect, odd communication, and social isolation. One heterozygote met full criteria for schizophrenia. Forty per cent of the heterozygotes also met diagnostic criteria for some form of chronic recurrent depressive disorder, which was usually a remitting, relapsing depression of mild to moderate severity. Both of the findings were significantly different from controls who were matched for SES and having a child with significant developmental delays.

Treatment

There is no cure for the fragile X syndrome but treatment options exist from a variety of professionals, and their help can be beneficial, particularly for children (Levitas *et al.* 1983). A team approach is most helpful for affected fragile X boys and girls, and it usually includes a special education teacher, a speech and language pathologist, an occupational therapist, a physician, a psychologist, and a genetic counsellor. After the diagnosis is made, the genetic counsellor or geneticist will explain the inheritance pattern to the immediate and extended family members. In many pedigrees this is no small task because of the large numbers of heterozygotes who are at risk of having affected children. The complexities of fragile X inheritance also complicate the counselling and the family's understanding of their risks. After the diagnosis is explained, it is helpful for parents to be in contact with other fragile X families to compare and verbalize their experiences, particularly in behaviour management. The National Fragile X Foundation (PO Box 300233, Denver, Colorado 80203) was established by fragile X families and seeks to network parent contacts internationally. They publish a quarterly newsletter with helpful information for both parents and professionals. New parents should be given their address as an additional source for support and information.

After the diagnosis, the teachers and therapists will create an educational programme, which should be modified by the diagnosis because of the pattern of neuropsychological strengths and weaknesses which are consistently seen in affected fragile X children (Chudley and Hagerman 1987; Hagerman 1987). The physician will follow the child medically for the clinical problems which are commonly associated with fragile X. The physician can also medically treat the behavioural problems which are common in fragile X.

Medical intervention

The behavioural problem which is most amenable to medication is hyperactivity. The Attention Deficit Hyperactivity Disorder (ADHD) is seen in almost all affected fragile X boys, (Fryns *et al.* 1984; Largo and Schnitzel 1985; Hagerman 1987). Hyperactivity is often the presenting complaint instead of retardation, and over 30 per cent of fragile X boys are treated with stimulant medication before the diagnosis of fragile X is made (Hagerman 1987).

CNS stimulants have been used for hyperactivity or ADHD since the 1940s (Bradley 1937). The most commonly used medications include methylphenidate, dextroamphetamine, and pemoline. Their chemical structure is similar to natural neurotransmitters and they act at the synapse of both dopaminergic and norepinephrine pathways. They stimulate neurotransmission across the synapse, and the resultant clinical effects include improved attention, enhanced appropriate inhibition, and a decrease in hyperactivity (Shaywitz and Shaywitz 1984).

In numerous clinical studies over the past three decades, the reported response rate for ADHD children to stimulant medication is 60–80 per cent (Taylor 1986). The side-effects of these medications include anorexia which, when poorly monitored, can lead to weight loss and a subsequent loss in height growth, although this is reversible when the medication is discontinued (Roche *et al.* 1979). If weight loss does not occur, height growth is unaffected. Stimulants can also cause cardiovascular stimulation such that heart rate and blood pressure must be monitored along with growth parameters at least once every six months.

In the past, stimulants were not considered helpful in retarded hyperactive children. Stimulants were thought to narrow the breadth of attention which is already too limited in the retarded child (Aman 1982). This is probably true for the moderately and severely retarded child, but evidence exists that stimulants may be helpful in the mildly retarded child (Alexandris and Lundell 1968; Blacklidge and Ekblad 1971). A double-blind, cross-over trial of methylphenidate, dextroamphetamine, and placebo was carried out in 15 prepubertal fragile X children who had ADHD, and two of whom were girls (Hagerman *et al.* 1988). In the group as a whole, a significant improvement was seen in the attention span and socialization skills of children treated with methylphenidate, as noted by the teacher's report. On an individual basis, 10 of the 15 patients clinically responded to the stimulants which were subsequently continued long-term. These preliminary results and previous anecdotal reports suggest that hyperactive or significantly inattentive fragile X boys or girls should be considered for a trial of stimulant medication. From our own experience, I would suggest a trial of methylphenidate in a relatively low dose, i.e. 0.3 mg/kg/dose, since fragile X children are sensitive to the side-effects, particularly mood lability.

Folic acid

The use of folic acid has a longer history than the use of stimulant medication in the treatment of fragile X individuals. Lejeune (1982) was the first to anecdotally describe its benefit in eight fragile X males. This report stimulated further studies, some controlled (Carpenter *et al.* 1983; Brown *et al.* 1984) and others not (Lacassie *et al.* 1984; Harpey 1982; Lejeune *et al.* 1984). Although the patient numbers are limited, many studies (Rosenblatt *et al.* 1985; Froster-Iskenius *et al.* 1986*b*; Madison *et al.* 1986*b*; Wells and Madison 1986) have reported no effect of folic acid, even with doses up to 250 mg/day (Brown *et al.* 1986*b*). Other studies have found that a limited number of children demonstrate improvements in hyperactivity, attentional problems, autistic characteristics, or language (Brown *et al.* 1984; Carpenter *et al.* 1983; Gustavson *et al.* 1985; Hagerman *et al.* 1986*a*). In our experience (Hagerman *et al.* 1986*a*) 25 fragile X males were treated in a double-blind, cross-over fashion with 10 mg of folic acid per day for six months compared to placebo for six months. Although the group as a whole did not demonstrate significant improvements in behaviour or cognitive abilities, several fragile X prepubertal boys demonstrated improvement in their hyperactivity and attention span. When the data from the eight prepubertal boys were analysed separately, there was a significant improvement in their cognitive abilities while taking folic acid compared to placebo. Clinically, this effect appeared to be secondary to the improvement in the ADHD symptoms.

There is evidence that a limited number of prepubertal fragile X boys may experience improvement in ADHD symptoms while taking folic acid. The effect is probably similar to the clinical effect of CNS stimulants, and preliminary studies suggest that the response rate to stimulants is better than the response rate to folic acid. Folate's effect is probably non-specific to fragile X, although its mechanism of action in the CNS is not clear. There is no known metabolic defect involving folate in fragile X syndrome (Brøndum-Nielsen *et al.* 1983*a*; Wang and Erbe 1984). However, there has also been a report that trimethoprim, an antibiotic that interferes with folic acid's metabolism, can cause a deterioration of behaviour and development in fragile X males (Hecht and Glover 1983).

Folate has relatively few side-effects and is well tolerated orally. It has been given in doses up to 1000 mg/day in normal volunteers without significant problems (Zettner *et al.* 1981). It can exacerbate the frequency of seizures in patients with epilepsy (Reynolds 1967), and approximately 20 per cent of males with fragile X syndrome have recurrent seizures. The typical doses used in treating fragile X patients range from 10 mg/day to 100 mg/day. At higher doses, loose stools or gastrointestinal discomfort can occasionally develop. Vitamin B_6 deficiency (by serum analysis) was seen in three of 25 study patients (Hagerman *et al.* 1986*a*) and can be avoided by starting a daily multiple vitamin which has B_6. Zinc deficiency can also occasionally be found in those taking large doses of folic acid, because folate interferes with zinc absorption in the gastrointestinal tract (Milne *et al.* 1984). The follow-up of patients on high doses of folic acid should include periodic blood work, including serum levels of vitamin B_6, zinc, folate, and a CBC, liver and renal studies, urinalysis, and a physical and neurologic examination at least once a year. Follow-up cognitive and behavioural testing is also helpful to evaluate the effectiveness of the treatment.

If folate is considered beneficial when started, then, approximately yearly or every other year, it should be discontinued for at least a two-month period to evaluate whether it continues to be worthwhile. There is limited evidence to suggest a mild withdrawal effect, characterized by mood lability, that can last a week or more after folate is discontinued. Withdrawal from mega-vitamin therapy has been described with pyridoxine and ascorbic acid (APA Task Force on Vitamin Therapy 1973), and this may be related to the induction of high levels of coenzymes and subsequent formation of apoenzymes which are unsaturated when the vitamin is discontinued (Gualtieri *et al.* 1987).

The use of other medications in fragile X syndrome have not been studied in a controlled fashion and only anecdotal information is available. Thioridazine, a major tranquillizer, has been helpful in many adult fragile X males to control aggressive outbursts and agitation. It has been widely used for similar reasons in both children and adults with retardation, autism, and pervasive developmental delays. It has relatively few side-effects compared to other neuroleptics (Mikkelson 1982). It does not, however, enhance cognitive abilities, and in higher doses it can cause the blunting of affect and somnolence. We have had limited experience with the use of lithium for control of aggressive outbursts in fragile X adult males. It has been remarkably beneficial in three patients. Fenfluramine has been helpful in decreasing hyperactivity and improving behaviour in one case with fragile X syndrome (Reiss *et al.* 1988*b*). Clonidine has been helpful in decreasing hyperactivity in three fragile X patients (Leckman 1987). Clearly, further knowledge of the neurochemical dysfunction in fragile X and more controlled studies of psychoactive drugs are needed to advance our knowledge of medical intervention.

Medical follow-up

The physical features of the fragile X syndrome include findings associated with a connective tissue dysplasia (Opitz *et al.* 1984). The most obvious findings seen in the majority of fragile X males are hyperextensible finger joints; large and prominent ears; and soft, velvety skin, especially in the hands (Hagerman *et al.* 1983; Opitz and Sutherland 1984). Other features related to a connective tissue dysplasia are seen in the majority of fragile X males but require more significant medical intervention. Severe pes planus with medial rotation of the ankle will often require orthotics and, rarely, surgery. Strabismus has been seen in up to 56 per cent of fragile X males and requires early detection and treatment to avoid amblyopia (Schinzel and Largo 1985; Storm *et al.* 1987). Since the clinical presentation may be subtle, a routine evaluation by an ophthalmologist by 4 years of age is recommended.

Recurrent otitis media is a frequent problem for fragile X males (Hagerman *et al.* 1987*a*). The long, narrow face and high-arched palate related to the connective tissue abnormalities in fragile X may predispose young children to eustachian tube dysfunction leading to recurrent otitis. In normal children, recurrent otitis can lead to verbal, cognitive, and articulation deficits (Zinkus *et al.* 1978). In the retarded population, attention to ear care and thus less otitis has been associated with a higher IQ (Saxon and Witriol 1976; Libb *et al.* 1985). In fragile X patients it is imperative to treat recurrent otitis media aggressively. Persistent serous otitis is a frequent sequela of purulent otitis and it often causes a mild to moderate conductive hearing loss. Such a problem, if prolonged, will cause further verbal disability in a syndrome which already experiences significant language dysfunction. If a persistent conductive hearing loss occurs in fragile X patients, the placement of polyethylene tubes in the tympanic membranes is indicated. The follow-up for treatment of otitis media should include an audiometric assessment to detect serous otitis and conductive hearing loss.

Other medical problems, such as hernia, scoliosis, cleft palate, and seizures, occur in a higher incidence than normal in fragile X patients. The routine physical examinations of fragile X patients should also include a careful cardiac examination. Mitral valve prolapse is present in approximately 50 per cent of males (Loehr *et al.* 1986), and this will occasionally include significant mitral regurgitation. If a murmur or click is present on cardiac examination, then consultation with a cardiologist is indicated. The cardiac evaluation should include an echocardiogram to further evaluate the mitral valve. If mitral valve prolapse or other cardiac abnormality is found, then subacute bacterial endocarditis (SBE) prophylaxis is indicated for dental procedures and surgery which could contaminate the bloodstream (McNamara 1982).

Only one case of sudden cardiac death has been reported in a fragile X male (Waldstein *et al.* 1988). The cause of death was an arrhythmia secondary to a viral myocarditis. Autopsy demonstrated a hypoplastic descending aorta, left ventricular hypertrophy, and abnormal mitral and tricuspid valves. The elastic fibres were abnormally fragmented and disorganized in the aorta, in the valves, and in the skin. This finding was similar to that previously reported in skin biopsies of several fragile X males (Waldstein *et al.* 1986). Perhaps there is an abnormality of elastin structure or organization in the fragile X syndrome which may occasionally lead to more significant malformations.

Educational intervention

The educational intervention for the fragile X syndrome always involves some form of special education help. For the high-functioning fragile X boys and affected heterozygotes this may only involve remediation in individualized or small group format, on a pull-out basis from the regular classroom. Most learning-disabled fragile X children have their greatest academic delay in mathematics. In those with lowered cognitive abilities, all of the other academic areas suffer, including reading and spelling, although mathematics usually remains the lowest in academic achievement. These children require a self-contained classroom with a limited number of children. Mainstreaming for non-academic subjects is beneficial for social patterning since many fragile X boys will imitate to a certain extent the behaviour to which they are exposed (Hagerman 1987).

In the mildly retarded or higher-functioning males, the academic achievement scores are usually higher than one would expect given the IQ level (Kemper *et al.* 1988). This is most easily demonstrated on the Kaufman Assessment Battery for Children (K-ABC), which is a relatively new IQ test. The scores include a Mental Processing Composite (MPC) score, which reflects the patient's ability to solve novel problems, and an Achievement Score, which reflects the level of learning from the environment, i.e. school and home. In a controlled study of 20 fragile X boys with an IQ above 50, almost all demonstrated a higher Achievement Score than MPC score. Consistencies were also seen in the way fragile X males processed information, specifically the Simultaneous Processing score of the MPC was almost always higher than the Sequential Processing score of the MCP. Similar findings were reported by Leckman (1987) and they suggest some general educational approaches for fragile X children. The strengths in Simultaneous Processing were secondary to high visual gestalt processing abilities. Fragile X children usually learn to read by memorizing the visual pattern of words and not by phonetic blending (Hagerman *et al.* 1985; Kemper *et al.* 1988). They have significant difficulty with the auditory processing of information. This difficulty relates to their attentional problems, impulsivity, and distractability. They have difficulty in focusing their attention on incoming auditory stimuli and in focusing their expressive language. Tangential remarks and poor topic maintenance are consistent problems for all verbal fragile X males and many affected heterozygotes (Hanson *et al.* 1986; Hagerman 1987). The use of CNS stimulant medication can be helpful for the distractibility and attentional problems, but language therapy is a necessity to improve both the receptive and expressive difficulties. Auditory processing, memory, sequencing, and word retrieval are all areas of deficit that can be addressed in a therapy programme which emphasizes better organization of verbal formulation. The sometimes exceptional ability of imitation that many fragile X males possess can be beneficial in therapy strategies that include role-playing.

Fragile X males have a great deal of difficulty in analysing information and creating unique solutions, or in generalizing what they learn. One mother stated to me that her moderately retarded son was taught to order from a menu but could only do so in the specific restaurant where this ability was originally taught. The educational programming must address this issue and present a variety of situations where a certain learned concept can be used. The understanding of mathematical concepts is also particularly difficult for fragile X males, perhaps because of the abstract concepts involved. For many fragile X boys, numbers are meaningless on paper because they cannot be translated into the environment. It is perhaps better to present mathematics in the context of everyday life, such as construction projects or cooking. Once the patient understands the meaning of four eggs and two cups of milk, the information can be generalized to other concrete objects. The creation of learning situations in the everyday environment helps the fragile X child retain and utilize the information in his own living experience.

For many fragile X males autistic characteristics, such as perseverative speech and stereotypes, interfere with learning. These children are easily overwhelmed in new situations or confusing circumstances and aggressive outbursts or tantrums may be a problem. Occupational therapy can be very helpful for these children by using calming techniques such as deep breathing, progressive relaxation, calming environmental music or sounds, and deep pressure or a vibrating pillow (Hickman 1987). Helping a fragile X child to recognize when he is beginning to be overwhelmed and to communicate this feeling will greatly facilitate the institution of a calming routine and the avoidance of a tantrum or outburst. These techniques will be helpful, not only for teachers, but also parents. The occupational therapist can also help with improving motor inco-ordination, joint instability, motor planning problems, and tactile defensiveness with sensory integration therapy.

Conclusion

We are just beginning to define the neurobehavioural phenotype of the fragile X syndrome. The information that has accumulated so far has guided us in new directions for medical and educational intervention. Further research in the neuropathology and neurochemistry of fragile X will help to initiate new and more effective treatments. The fragile X syndrome will also bring the field of behavioural sciences closer to understanding the genetic and organic aspects of psychopathology. This syndrome has initiated the subtyping of autism and will, hopefully, eventually clarify the neurochemical dysfunction in this disorder. We are coming ever closer to understanding how the chromosomes affect the neurodevelopmental process that leads to behaviour and cognition.

References

Alexandris, A. and Lundell, F. W. (1968). Effect of thioridazine, amphetamine and placebo on the hyperkinetic syndrome and cognitive area in mentally deficient children. *Canadian Medical Association Journal*, **98**, 92–6.

Aman, M. G. (1982). Stimulant drug effects in developmental disorders and hyperactivity—toward a resolution of disparate findings. *Journal of Autism and Development Disorders*, **12**, 385–98.

American Psychiatric Association (1980). *Diagnostic and statistical manual (DSM III)*, pp. 88–90. Washington, DC.

American Psychiatric Association (1973). *APA task force on vitamin therapy in psychiatry: megavitamin and orthomolecular therapy in psychiatry.* Washington, D.C.

Blacklidge, V. and Ekblad, R. L. (1971). The effectiveness of methylphenidate hydrochloride (Ritalin) on learning and behavior in public school educable mentally retarded children. *Pediatrics*, **47**, 923–6.

Bradley, C. (1937). The behavior of children receiving benzedrine. *American Journal of Psychiatry*, **94**, 557–85.

Brøndum-Nielsen, K., Tommerup, N., Frilis, B., Hjelt, K. and Hippe, E. (1983*a*). Folic acid metabolism in a patient with fragile X. *Clinical Genetics*, **24**, 153–5.

Brown, W. T. *et al.* (1982). Autism is associated with the fragile X syndrome. *Journal of Autism and Development Disorders*, **12**, 303–7.

Brown, W. T. *et al.* (1984). Folic acid therapy in the fragile X syndrome. *American Journal of Medical Genetics*, **17**, 289–97.

Brown, W. T. *et al.* (1986*a*). Fragile X and autism: a multicenter survey. *American Journal of Medical Genetics*, **23**, 341–52.

Brown, W. T. *et al.* (1986*b*). High dose folic acid treatment of fragile X males. *American Journal of Medical Genetics*, **23**, 263–71.

Carpenter, N. J., Barber, D. H., Jones, M., Lindley, W., and Carr, C. (1983). Controlled six-month study of oral folic acid therapy in boys with fragile X-linked mental retardation. *American Journal of Human Genetics*, **35**, supplement.

Chudley, A. E. and Hagerman, R. J. (1987). Fragile X syndrome. *Journal of Pediatrics*, **110**, 821–31.

Chudley, A. E., Knoll, J., Gerrard, J. W., Shepel, L., McGahey, E., and Anderson, J. (1983). Fragile (X) X-linked mental retardation. I: Relationship between age and intelligence and the frequency of expression of fragile (X)(q28). *American Journal of Medical Genetics*, **14**, 699–712.

Cohen, I. L. *et al.* (1988). Social gaze, social avoidance and repetitive behavior in fragile X males: a controlled study. *American Journal of Mental Retardation*, **92**, 436–46.

Conners, C. K. (1973). Rating scales for use in drug studies with children. *Psychopharmacology Bulletin*, Special Issue, 24–84, 219–22.

Daker, M. G., Chidiac, P., Fear, C. N., and Berry, A. C. (1981). Fragile X in a normal male: a cautionary tale. *Lancet*, **i**, 780.

Edwards, D. R., Keppen, L. D., and Gollin, S. M. (1987). *Autism and fragile X syndrome.* Poster presentation at the First National Fragile X Conference, Fragile X Foundation. Denver, Colorado, 3–4 December.

Finnelli, P. F., Pueschel, S. M., Pade-Mendoza, T., and O'Brien, M. M. (1985). Neurological findings in patients with the fragile X syndrome. *Journal of Neurology Neurosurgery and Psychiatry*, **48**, 150–3.

Fisher, M. A. and Zeaman, D. (1970). Growth and decline of retardate intelligence. In *International review of research in mental retardation*, Vol. 4, (ed. N. R. Ellis), pp. 151–92. Academic Press, New York.

Froster-Iskenius, U., McGillivray, B. C., Dill, F. J., Hall, J. G., and Herbst, D. S. (1986*a*). Normal male carriers in the fra(X) form of X-linked mental retardation (Martin–Bell syndrome). *American Journal of Medical Genetics*, **23**, 619–31.

Froster-Iskenius, U., Bodeker, K., Oepen, T., Matthes, R., Piper, U. and Schwinger, E. (1986*b*). Folic acid treatment of males and females with fragile X syndrome. *American Journal of Medical Genetics*, **23**, 273–89.

Fryns, J. P. (1986). The female and the fragile X: a study of 144 obligate female carriers. *American Journal of Medical Genetics*, **23**, 157–69.

Fryns, J. P., Jacob, J., Kleczkowska, A., and van den Berghe, H. (1984). The psychological profile of the fragile X syndrome. *Clinical Genetics*, **25**, 131–4.

Goldfine, P. E., McPherson, D. M., Hardesty, V. A., Heath, G. A., Beauregard, L. J., and Baker, A. A. (1987). Fragile X chromsome associated with primary learning disability. *Journal of the American Academy of Child Psychiatry*, **26**, 589–92.

Grigsby, J., Kemper, M. B., and Hagerman, R. J. (1987). Developmental Gerstmann syndrome without aphasia in fragile X syndrome. *Neuropsychologia*, **25**, (6), 881–91.

Gualtieri, T., Evans, R. W., and Patterson, D. R. (1987). The medical treatment of autistic people: Problems and side effects. In *Neurobiological issues in autism*, (ed. E. Shapler and G. B. Mesibov). Plenum Publishing, New York.

Gustavson, K. H., Dahlborn, K., Flood, A., Holmgren, G., and Blomquist, H. K. (1985). Effect of folic acid treatment in the fragile X syndrome. *Clinical Genetics*, **27**, 463–7.

Hagerman, R. J. (1987). Fragile X syndrome. *Current Problems in Pediatrics*, **17**, 623–74.

Hagerman, R. J. and Smith, A. C. M. (1983). The heterozygous female. In *The fragile X syndrome: diagnosis, biochemistry and intervention*, (ed. R. J. Hagerman and P. M. McBogg), pp. 83–94. Spectra Publishing, Dillon, Colorado.

Hagerman, R., Smith, A. C. M., and Mariner, R. (1983). Clinical features of the fragile X syndrome. In *The fragile X syndrome: diagnosis, biochemistry, and intervention*, (ed. R. J. Hagerman and P. McBogg), pp. 17–53. Dillon, Colorado.

Hagerman, R. J., Kemper, M., and Hudson, M. (1985). Learning disabilities and attentional problems in boys with the fragile X syndrome. *American Journal of Diseases of Children*, **139**, 674–8.

Hagerman, R. J. *et al.* (1986*a*). Oral folic acid versus placebo in the treatment of males with the fragile X syndrome. *American Journal of Medical Genetics*, **23**, 241–62.

Hagerman, R. J., Jackson, A. W., Levitas, A., Rimland, B., and Braden, M. (1986*b*). An analysis of autism in 50 males with the fragile X syndrome. *American Journal of Medical Genetics*, **23**, 359–74.

Hagerman, R. J., Chudley, A. E., Knoll, J. H., Jackson, A. W., Kemper, M., and Ahmad, R. (1986*c*). Autism in fragile X females. *American Journal of Medical Genetics*, **23**, 375–80.

Hagerman, R. J., Altshul-Stark, D., and McBogg, P. (1987*a*). Recurrent otitis media in boys with the fragile X syndrome. *American Journal of Diseases of Children*, **141**, 184–7.

Hagerman, R. J., Schreiner, R., Habicht, K., Kemper, M., and Wittenberger, M. (1987*b*). *Longitudinal IQ changes in fragile X males.* First National Fragile X Conference, Fragile X Foundation, Denver, Colorado, 3–4 December.

Hagerman, R. J., Murphy, M. A., and Wittenberger, M. D. (1988). A controlled trial of stimulant medication in children with the fragile X syndrome. *American Journal of Medical Genetics*, **30**, 377–92.

Hanson, D. M., Jackson, A. W., and Hagerman, R. J. (1986). Speech disturbances (cluttering) in mildly impaired males with the Martin–Bell/Fragile X syndrome. *American Journal of Medical Genetics*, **23**, 195–206.

Harpey, J. P. (1982). Treatment of fragile X (letter). *Pediatrics*, **69**, 670.

Hecht, F. and Glover, T. W. (1983). Antibiotics containing trimethoprim and the fragile X chromosome (letter). *New England Journal of Medicine*, **308**, 285.

Herbst, D., Dunn, G., Dill, F., Kalousek, D., and Keywanick, L. (1981). Further delineation of X-linked mental retardation. *Human Genetics*, **58**, 366–72.

Hickman, L. (1987). *Calming techniques for parents, educators and therapists.* First National Fragile X Conference, Fragile X Foundation, Denver, Colorado, 3–4 December.

Howard-Peebles, D. and Friedman, J. M. (1985). Unaffected carrier males in families with fragile X syndrome. *American Journal of Human Genetics*, **37**, 956–64.

Howard-Peebles, P. N., Stoddard, G. R., and Mims, M. (1979). Familial X-linked mental retardation, verbal disability and marker X chromosomes. *American Journal of Human Genetics*, **31**, 214–22.

Jacobs, P. *et al.* (1980). X-linked mental retardation: A study of seven families. *American Journal of Medical Genetics*, **14**, 713.

Kemper, M. B., Hagerman, R. J., Ahmad, R. S., and Mahner, R. (1986). Cognitive profiles and the spectrum of clinical manifestations in heterozygous fra (X) females. *American Journal of Medical Genetics*, **23**, 139–56.

Kemper, M. B., Hagerman, R. J., and Altshul-Stark, D. (1988). Cognitive profiles of boys with the fragile X syndrome. *American Journal of Medical Genetics*, **30**, 191–200.

Lacassie, Y., Curotto, B., Alliende, M. A., de Andraca, I., and Zavala, A. (1984). Evaluacion prelminar del tratamienton con acido folico en dos pacientes con retrasco mental ligado al sexo y macroorquidismo. *Revista Medica de Chile (Santiago)*, **112**, 469–73.

Lachiewicz, A. M., Gullion, C. M., Spiridigliozzi, G. A., and Aylsworth, A. S.

(1987). Declining IQ scores of young males with fragile X syndrome. *American Journal of Mental Retardation*, **92**, 272–8.

Largo, R. H. and Schinzel, A. (1985). Developmental and behavioral disturbances in 13 boys with fragile X syndrome. *European Journal of Pediatrics*, **143**, 269–75.

Leckman, J. (1987). *Cognitive and neuropsychological features of the fragile X syndrome*. First National Fragile X Conference, Fragile X Foundation, Denver, Colorado, 3–4 December.

Leckman, J., Hodapp, R. M., and Dykens, E. (1987). *The trajectory of IQ in fragile X males*. First National Fragile X Conference, Fragile X Foundation, Denver, Colorado, 3–4 December.

Lejeune, J. (1982). Is the fragile X syndrome amenable to treatment? (letter). *Lancet*, **i**, 273–4.

Lejeune, J., Rethoré, M.-O., de Blois, M.-C., and Ravel, A. (1984). Assay of folic acid treatment in fragile-X syndrome. *Annales de Génétique*, **27**, (4), 230–2.

Levitas, A., Braden, M., Van Norman, K., Hagerman, R. J., and McBogg, P. M. (1983). Treatment and intervention. In *The fragile X syndrome: diagnosis, biochemistry and intervention*, (ed. R. J. Hagerman and P. M. McBogg), pp. 153–73. Spectra Publishing, Denver, Colorado.

Libb, J. W., Dahle, A., Smith, K., McCollister, F. P., and McLain, C. (1985). Hearing disorder and cognitive function of individuals with Down syndrome. *American Journal of Mental Deficiency*, **90**, 353–6.

Loehr, J. P., Synhorst, D. P., Wolfe, R. R., and Hagerman, R. J. (1986). Aortic root dilatation and mitral valve prolapse in the fragile X syndrome. *American Journal of Medical Genetics*, **23**, 189–94.

Loesch, D. Z., Hay, D. A., Sutherland, G. R., Halliday, J., Judge, C., and Webb, G. C. (1987). Phenotypic variation in male-transmitted fragile X: genetic inferences. *American Journal of Medical Genetics*, **27**, 401–17.

Madison, L. S., George, C., and Moeschler, J. B. (1986*a*). Cognitive functioning in the fragile X syndrome: a study of intellectual, memory and communications skills. *Journal of Mental Deficiency Research*, **30**, 129–48.

Madison, L. S., Wells, T. E., Fristo, T. E., and Benesch, C. G. (1986*b*). A controlled study of folic acid treatment in 3 fragile X syndrome males. *Journal of Developmental and Behavioural Pediatrics*, **7**, 253–6.

Mattei, J. F., Mattei, M. G., Aumeras, C., Auger, M., and Giraud, F. (1981). X-linked mental retardation with the fragile X. A study of 15 families. *Human Genetics*, **59**, 281–9.

McNamara, D. G. (1982). Idiopathic benign mitral valve prolapse: the pediatrician's view. *American Journal of Diseases of Children*, **136**, 152–6.

Miezejeski, C. M., Jenkins, E. C., Hill, A. L., Wisniewski, K., French, J. H., and Brown, T. W. (1986). A profile of cognitive deficit in females from fragile X families. *Neuropsychologia*, **24**, 405–9.

Mikkelson, E. J. (1982). Efficacy of neuroleptic medication in pervasive developmental disorders of childhood. *Schizophrenia Bulletin*, **8**, 320–32.

Milne, D. B., Canfield, W. K., Mahalko, J. R., and Sandstead, H. H. (1984). Effect of oral folic acid supplements on zinc, copper and iron absorption and excretion. *American Journal of Clinical Nutrition*, **39**, 535–9.

Newell, K., Sanborn, B., and Hagerman, R. J. (1983). Speech and language dysfunction in the fragile X syndrome. In *The fragile X syndrome: diagnosis, biochemistry and intervention*, (ed. R. J. Hagerman and P. M. McBogg), pp. 175–200. Spectra Publishing, Dillon, Colorado.

Opitz, J. M. and Sutherland, G. R. (1984). Conference report: International workshop on the fragile X and X-linked mental retardation. *American Journal of Medical Genetics*, **17**, 5–94.

Opitz, J. M., Westphal, J. M., and Daniel, A. (1984). Discovery of a connective tissue dysplasia in the Martin–Bell syndrome. *American Journal of Medical Genetics*, **17**, 101–9.

Ornitz, E. M. and Ritvo, E. R. (1968). Perceptual inconstancy in early infantile autism. *Archives of General Psychiatry*, **18**, 76–98.

Partington, M. W. (1984). The fragile X syndrome II: Preliminary data on growth and development in males. *American Journal of Medical Genetics*, **17**, 175–94.

Paul, R., Cohen, D. J., Breg, W. R., Watson, M., and Herman, S. (1984). Fragile X syndrome: its relation to speech and language disorders (letter). *Journal of Speech and Hearing Disorders*, **49**, 328–32.

Reiss, A. and Patel, S. (1987). *Magnetic resonance imaging of the central nervous system in fragile X males.* First National Fragile X Conference, Fragile X Foundation, Denver, Colorado, 3–4 December.

Reiss, A. L., Hagerman, R. J., Vinogradov, S., Abrams, M., and King, R. (1988*a*). Psychiatric disability in female carriers of the fragile X chromosome. *Archives of General Psychiatry*, **45**, 25–30.

Reiss, A. L., Egel, A. L., Feinstein, C., and Goldsmith Boiengassar-Caruso, M. A. (1988*b*). Effects of fenfluoramine on social behavior in autistic children. *Journal of Autism and Development Disorders*, in press.

Reynolds, E. H. (1967). Effects of folic acid on the mental state and fit frequency of drug treated epileptic patients. *Lancet*, **i**, 1086–8.

Roche, A. F., Lipman, R. S., Overall, J. E., and Hung, W. (1979). The effects of stimulant medication on the growth of hyperkinetic children. *Pediatrics*, **63**, 847–50.

Rosenblatt, D. S. *et al.* (1985). Folic acid blinded trial in identical twins with fragile X syndrome. *American Journal of Human Genetics*, **37**, 543–52.

Saxon, S. A. and Witriol, E. (1976). Down's syndrome and intellectual development. *Journal of Pediatric Psychology (New York)*, **1**, 45–7.

Schinzel, A. and Largo, R. H. (1985). The fragile X syndrome (Martin–Bell syndrome) clinical and cytogenetic findings in 16 prepubertal boys and in 4 of their 5 families. *Helvetica Paediatrica Acta*, **40**, 133–52.

Shaywitz, S. E. and Shaywitz, B. A. (1984). Neurochemical correlates of Attention Deficit Disorder. *Pediatric Clinics of North America*, **31**, 387–97.

Sherman, S. L. *et al.* (1984). The marker (X) syndrome: a cytogenetic and genetic analysis. *Annals of Human Genetics*, **48**, 21–37.

Sherman, S. L. *et al.* (1985). Further segregation analysis of the fragile X syndrome with special reference to transmitting males. *Human Genetics*, **69**, 289–99.

Storm, R. L., DeBenito, R., and Ferretti, C. (1987). The ophthalmologic findings in the fragile X syndrome. *Archives of Ophthalmology*, **105**, 1099–102.

Taylor, E. (1986). The basis of drug treatment. In *The overactive child*, (ed. E. Taylor), pp. 192–218. Spastics International Medical Publications, Oxford.

Theobold, T. M., Hay, D. A., and Judge, C. (1987). Individual variation and specific cognitive deficits in the Fra (X) syndrome. *American Journal of Medical Genetics*, **28**, 1–11.

Turner, G., Daniel, A., and Frost, M. (1980). X-linked mental retardation, macro-orchidism, and the Xq27 fragile site. *Journal of Pediatrics*, **96**, 837–41.

Veenema, H., Veenema, T., and Geraedts, J. P. M. (1987). The fragile X syndrome in a large family: II. Psychological investigations. *Journal of Medical Genetics*, **24**, 32–8.

Waldstein, G., Mierau, G., Ahmad, R., Thibodeau, S. N., Hagerman, R. J., and Caldwell, S. (1986). Fragile X syndrome: skin elastin abnormalities. *Genetic aspects of developmental pathology*, (ed. E. F. Gilbert and J. M. Opitz), pp. 103–14. Alan R. Liss, Inc., New York.

Waldstein, G., Hagerman, R., and Dawson, D. L. (1988). Aortic hypoplasia and cardiac valvular abnormalities in a young male with fragile X syndrome. *American Journal of Medical Genetics*, **30**, 83–98.

Wang, J. and Erbe, R. W. (1984). Folate metabolism in cells from fragile X syndrome patients and carriers. *American Journal of Medical Genetics*, **17**, 303–10.

Webb, T. P., Thake, A., and Todd, J. (1986). Twelve families with fragile X(q27). *Journal of Medical Genetics*, **23**, (5), 400–6.

Wells, T. E. and Madison, L. S. (1986). Assessment of behavior change in a fragile-X syndrome male treated with folic acid. *American Journal of Medical Genetics*, **23**, 291–6.

Wolff, P. H., Gardner, J., Lappen, J., Paccia, J., and Meryash, D. (1988). Variable expression of the fragile X syndrome in heterozygous females of normal intelligence. *American Journal of Medical Genetics*, **30**, 213–25.

Wolf-Schein, E. G. *et al.* (1987). Speech, language and the fragile X syndrome: Initial findings. *American Speech and Hearing Association*, **29**, 35–8.

Zettner, A., Boss, G., and Seegmiller, J. E. (1981). A long-term study of the absorption of large doses of folic acid. *Annals of Clinical and Laboratory Science*, **11**, 517–24.

Zinkus, P. W., Gottlieb, M. I., and Shapiro, M. (1978). Developmental and psychoeducational sequelae of chronic otitis media. *American Journal of Diseases of Children*, **132**, 1100–4.

4 DNA studies of the fragile X mutation

W. TED BROWN

Introduction

The molecular nature of the mutation underlying the fragile X syndrome is unknown. No specific abnormal gene or gene product has been identified. Lacking knowledge about which specific candidate genes might be involved, only indirect approaches have been available to identify and characterize the underlying mutation. Using DNA probes, the location of the mutation has been genetically mapped. Linked DNA probes have been useful for tracing the inheritance of the X chromosome within a family. They have been used for carrier detection, for detecting the presence of transmitting males, for assisting with prenatal diagnosis, and for studies of the nature of the underlying mutation. Having closely linked DNA markers allows for the use of new technologies to be used to undertake the isolation and characterization of the fragile X mutation. In this chapter, DNA linkage studies, hypotheses, and molecular investigations of the fragile X locus (*FRAXA*) will be reviewed.

Restriction fragment length polymorphisms and fragile X

A number of X-chromosome-specific DNA segments have been cloned and mapped relative to the fragile X locus. These probes identify DNA sequence variations between people which are inherited. Such variations can be detected by the use of restriction enzymes, and appear as variations in fragment lengths, hence they are known as *restriction fragment length polymorphisms* (RFLPs). The inheritance of RFLPs near to the fragile X site can be traced within families. RFLPs usually exist in one of two possible variations called *alleles* which are identified by numbers or letters. If a carrier mother has both type alleles of a given polymorphism, i.e. 1 and 2, she is termed a *heterozygote* for that polymorphism. Otherwise, she is a *homozygote*. It is necessary for a mother to be a heterozygote to be informative for the inheritance of a given X-linked polymorphism. The sons and daughters of a carrier mother receive one or the other of her two X chromosomes. If the mother is heterozygous for a given polymorphism, her sons and daughters will receive one or the other of the two alleles and inheritance of a given allele can be correlated with the inheritance of the fragile X locus.

Clinical use of RFLP DNA markers has become quite useful for risk assessment of carrier status (Brown *et al.* 1987*a*). If a DNA polymorphism is closely linked to the fragile X locus, then when a given allele is identified in a male with fragile X, it is very likely that siblings with the same allele will also inherit the fragile X chromosome. This can occur even though the fragile site itself may not be physically detectable or expressed, such as in the case of transmitting males and some carrier females. Likewise, those who inherit the opposite allele are unlikely to be carriers. Depending upon the distance along the chromosome between the RFLP and the fragile X locus, there is a certain probability of recombination occurring with each offspring. This distance is measured in terms of percentage recombination or recombinant fraction.

RFLPs and linkage studies

The first RFLP linked to the fragile X locus was clotting factor 9 (F9). Deficiency of this clotting factor is seen in haemophilia B or Christmas Disease. A large fragile X family was studied by Camerino *et al.* (1983) in which there were no recombinants seen and apparent tight linkage of the RFLP to the fragile X locus was observed. However, several families were soon reported by other investigators in which recombination was seen between F9 and the fragile X locus (Choo *et al.* 1984; Davies *et al.* 1985; Forster-Gibson *et al.* 1985; Warren *et al.* 1985; Zoll *et al.* 1985). We also observed several families such as the one illustrated in Fig. 4.1 which showed a high rate of recombination. In other families, such as illustrated in Figs 4.2 and 4.3, we noted very little recombination between F9 and fragile X. These striking differences in rates of recombination suggested the presence of genetic linkage heterogeneity.

When we first studied F9 linkage to fragile X in eight families and combined our results with those of eight published families, there appeared to be two types of fragile X families, those in which there was no recombination and those in which there was a high rate of recombination (Brown *et al.* 1985). Since several of the families with no recombination had non-penetrant (NP) or transmitting male (TM) grandfathers, it seemed likely that the presence or absence of a NP male was a

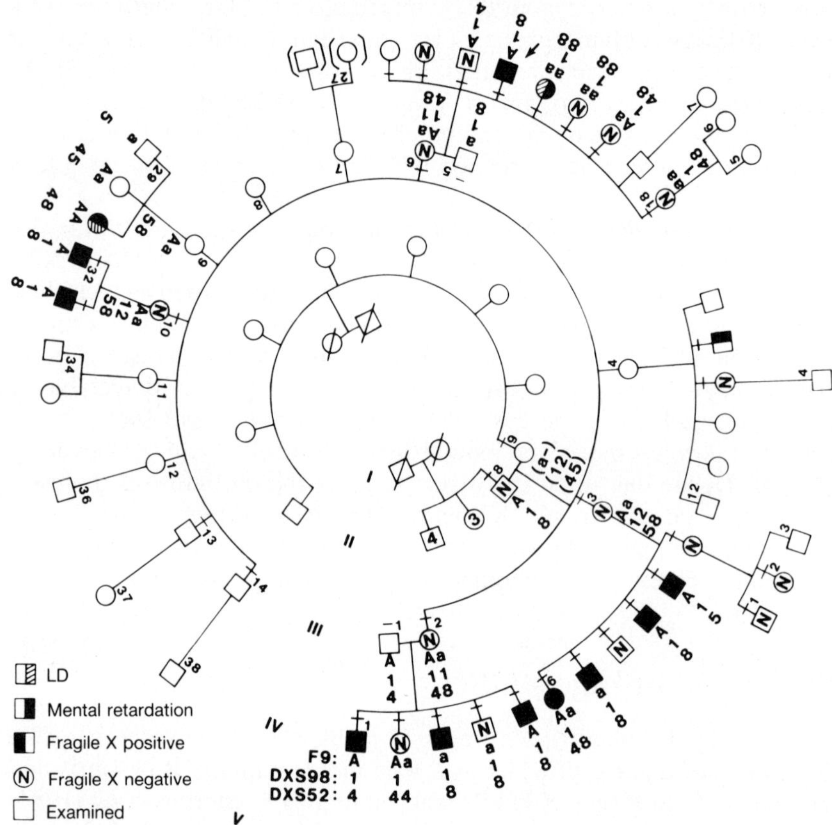

Fig. 4.1. A fragile X family (F20) which showed frequent recombination between F9 and fragile X (Brown *et al.* 1985, 1986, 1987*b*). Following risk analysis, the grandfather was identified as being a transmitting male since he had alleles A, 1, and 8 in common with the majority of his affected grandsons.

distinguishing factor. We therefore divided the families into two types, those with and those without an identified NP male, and used the 'predivided' sample statistic. This showed significant linkage heterogeneity, and we concluded there were two types of families; one with tight linkage to F9 and one with loose linkage.

Several other probes were soon reported to detect loci close to the fragile X locus. A highly polymorphic probe, St14, which detects locus DXS52, was found by Oberle *et al.* (1985*a*) to exist in approximately 10 different allelic types and to be close to fragile X (Oberle *et al.* 1986). Two other random DNA fragments including 52A (DXS51) and DX13 (DXS15) were found to be close to fragile X (Davies *et al.* 1985; Drayna

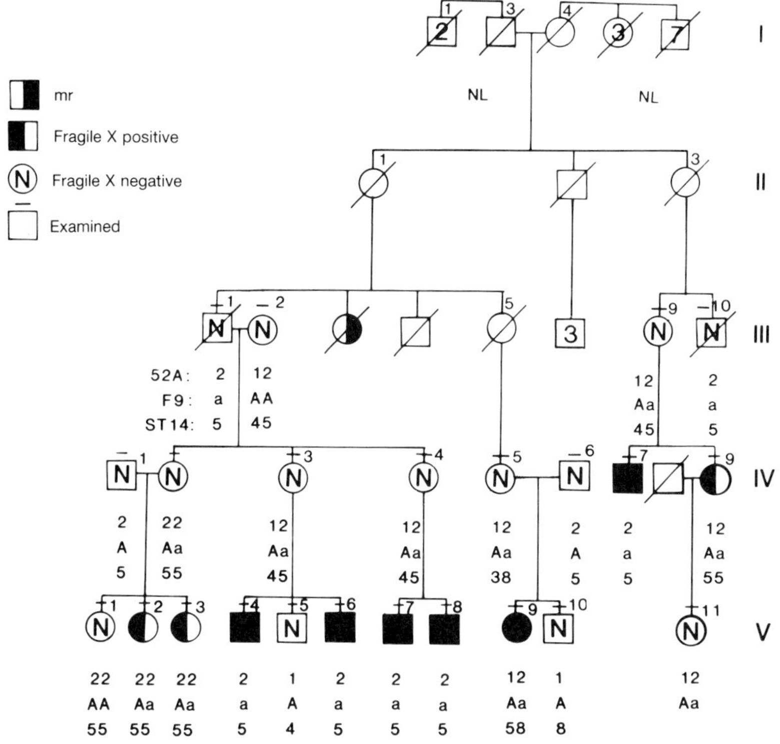

Fig. 4.2. A fragile X family (F22) which showed tight linkage between F9 and fragile X (Brown *et al.* 1985, 1986, 1987*b*). The grandfather (III-1) was a normal transmitting male since he had affected grandsons, and relatives of his mother and a sister were fragile X positive.

and White 1985). Following our initial studies of linkage with F9 we analysed 16 fragile X pedigrees for the inheritance of the RFLPs associated with 52A, F9, and St14. We combined this information with that published on 16 other fragile X pedigrees (Brown *et al.* 1986). In these 32 families, we again saw linkage heterogeneity for F9–fragile X. Based on the combined data, we again concluded that in families where NP males had been identified, a much lower rate of recombination between F9 and fragile X was likely than in other fragile X families where only penetrant males had been identified. We did not find heterogeneity for fragile X–St14 or 52A–F9.

Further studies of additional families and analysis of St14 inheritance patterns led us to conclude that non-penetrance was not a correct basis for division of families into two types (Brown *et al.* 1987*b*). Rather, some families appeared to show tight linkage and others showed loose

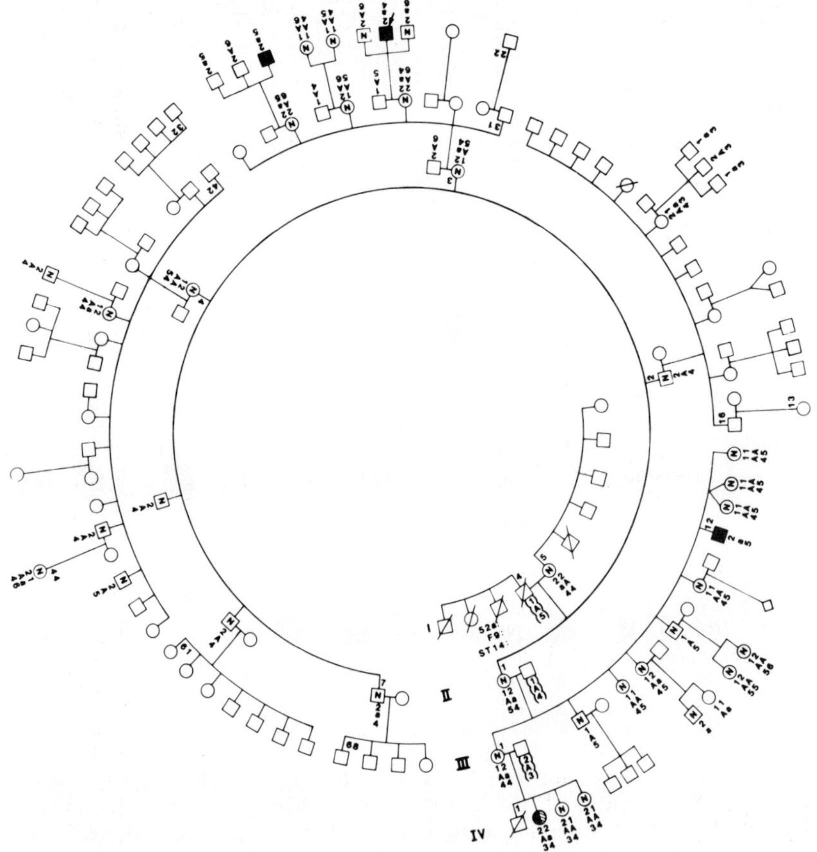

Fig. 4.3. A fragile X family (F52) which showed tight linkage between F9 and fragile X (Brown *et al.* 1987*b*). In this family the grandmother (I-5) was most likely a carrier since she had the alleles that her affected grandson and most of the affected great-grandchildren had inherited. Several likely non-penetrant males were identified (II-7, III-24, III-31).

linkage regardless of the presence of NP males in the family. We analysed DNA for RFLPs associated with 52A, F9, and St14 from 327 individuals belonging to 23 families segregating the fragile X chromosome. We combined this with published information on F9 in 27 families, 52A in six families, and St14 in five families. The LOD scores for two-point recombinations between the adjacent loci 52A–F9, F9–fragile X, and fragile X–St14 for 50 families are illustrated in Fig. 4.4.

As shown, there appeared to be wide variation in the recombination rate for F9–fragile X, much more than for fragile X–St14 or 52A–F9.

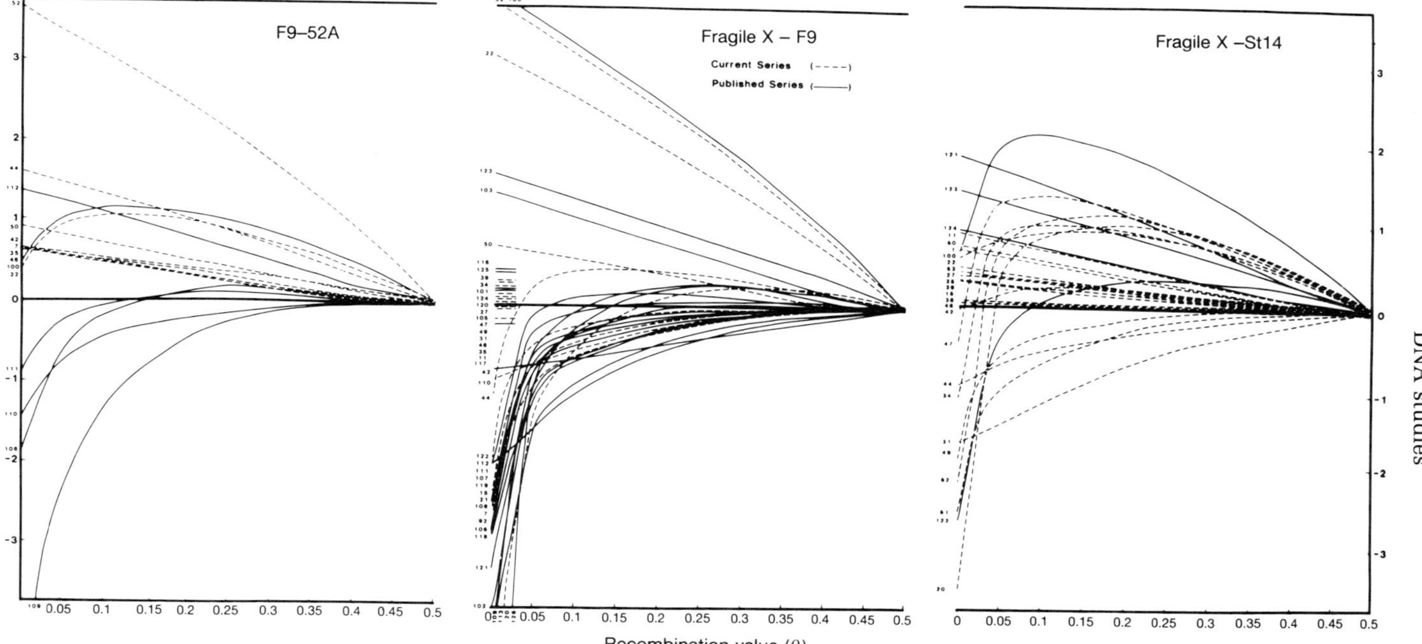

Fig. 4.4. Recombination values for two-point crosses between adjacent loci (Brown *et al.* 1987*b*). Some families showed tight linkage for F9 and fragile X with no recombinants, while others showed frequent recombination. Family F52 (Fig. 4.3) showed tight linkage with no recombination between either 52A–F9, or F9–fragile X. The one family with a high rate of recombination for 52A–F9 is that described by Veenema *et al.* (1987).

Some families showed no fragile X–F9 recombination, while others showed frequent recombination. Tests of linkage heterogeneity including the Morton test, the predivided test, and the Admixture test were employed. Although we initially divided families on the basis of whether or not an NP Male was identified and found significant linkage heterogeneity when the predivided sample statistic was used, our further analysis showed that many families which included a NP male also showed a high rate of F9–fragile X recombination. Thus, presence or absence of a NP male seemed unlikely to be related to the genetic heterogeneity observed and could not be used as a basis for predividing families in two categories.

The Morton linkage heterogeneity test is useful when a small number of large families are analysed. When large numbers of small families are also included the test results are often not significant, because little linkage information is contributed by increasing the number of uninformative families whereas the degrees of freedom are increased, and the power of the test decreases rapidly. Therefore, the Admixture test appeared to be the most useful and, in general, the most powerful test to employ for tests of linkage heterogeneity. We used the Admixture test to analyse our findings in two ways: Test 1 to test for linkage v. non-linkage, and Test 2 to look for tight linkage v. loose linkage (Brown *et al.* 1987*b*). Significant linkage heterogeneity between F9 and fragile X was found using Test 1 at $P < 0.0025$. When Test 2 was applied to F9–fragile X linkage the result gave a more significant value of $P < 0.0005$. The proportion (α) that showed loose linkage was about 0.76, with a peak LOD score at about 35 per cent recombination, and the proportion showing tight linkage was about 24 per cent. No significant linkage heterogeneity was found for other two-point linkages.

Although our results indicated two classes of families with two specific recombination rates (0 and 35 per cent), it seemed possible that actually there existed two distributions of recombination rates, one close to 0 and one averaging around 35 per cent. N. Risch developed a heterogeneity test which allows a test of this model. Our data was analysed by Risch using a new heterogeneity test, the Beta test, which statistically compares distributions. He found that results showed linkage heterogeneity with a slightly higher significance than the Admixture test (Risch 1988).

Our calculations of linkage used the value of 0.8 for penetrance in males based upon the segregation analysis of Sherman *et al.* (Sherman *et al.* 1984; Sherman *et al.* 1985). We considered it was possible that the penetrance might be higher or lower in different generations or in different pedigrees. We therefore tried different values of penetrance which gave us slightly different estimates of recombination fractions and peak LOD scores for F9–fragile X but did not alter the general conclusions. If there were no NP males identified in a particular family, increasing the penetrance estimate increased the overall LOD score between fragile X and other loci. However, if there were apparent NP males, increasing the penetrance increased the estimated recombinant fractions and decreased the LOD scores. As an example, family 52, illustrated in Fig. 4.3, had several suspected carrier males. A maximum LOD score of 3.4 at a recombinant fraction of 0 was found for fragile X–F9 when a penetrance of 0.8 was used. Increasing the penetrance from 0.8 to 0.9 increased the peak recombinant fraction to 0.03 and decreased the maximum LOD to 3.1, while increasing the penetrance to 0.95 produced a maximum LOD of 2.87 at 0.08.

Once there is good evidence of heterogeneity in a recombinant fraction, a problem arises as to how to firmly identify which families belong to the tightly or the loosely linked classes. It is clearly impossible to classify small nuclear families, unless recombination is seen. Families could be divided into tightly linked pedigrees and loosely linked pedigrees based on the prior probability of tight linkage to F9. As suggested by Ott (1985) an optimal rule may be to classify those families as linked where the posterior probability of linkage is greater than 0.5. Of 45 families where F9–fragile X linkage information was available, there were nine families with posterior probability of >0.7 for tight linkage. There were 18 families with a probability of <0.01 of tight linkage. The rest fell in an intermediate zone and could not be firmly classified. If families were divided into two classes based on either a prior probability of >70 per cent or <1 per cent for tight linkage, we were able to construct secondary recombinational maps for each class of families, as illustrated in Fig. 4.5.

DNA studies have been conducted on a number of other fragile X families by various laboratories (Landoulsi *et al.* 1985; Mulligan *et al.* 1985; Oberle *et al.* 1985*b*; Forster-Gibson *et al.* 1986; Goonewardena *et al.* 1986; Conner *et al.* 1987; Giannelli *et al.* 1987; Oberle *et al.* 1987). Giannelli *et al.* also reported finding F9–fragile X linkage heterogeneity which they associated with non-penetrance (Giannelli *et al.* 1987). We performed a combined multipoint analysis of 147 fragile X pedigrees with four flanking DNA markers, including information from 14 collaborating laboratories (Brown *et al.* 1988*a*). The four probes employed include F9, 52A (DXS51), St14 (DXS52), and DX13 (DXS15). Among the 147 pedigrees, there were 2030 individuals entered in the analysis, of which 1579 were typed for DNA markers. There were 693 fragile X positive males of which 595 were typed. Not all families were typed for each of the markers, and not all families were informative. There were 106 families informative for F9, 109 for St14, 53 for 52A, and 45 for DX13. Multipoint linkage analysis was performed using the LINKAGE

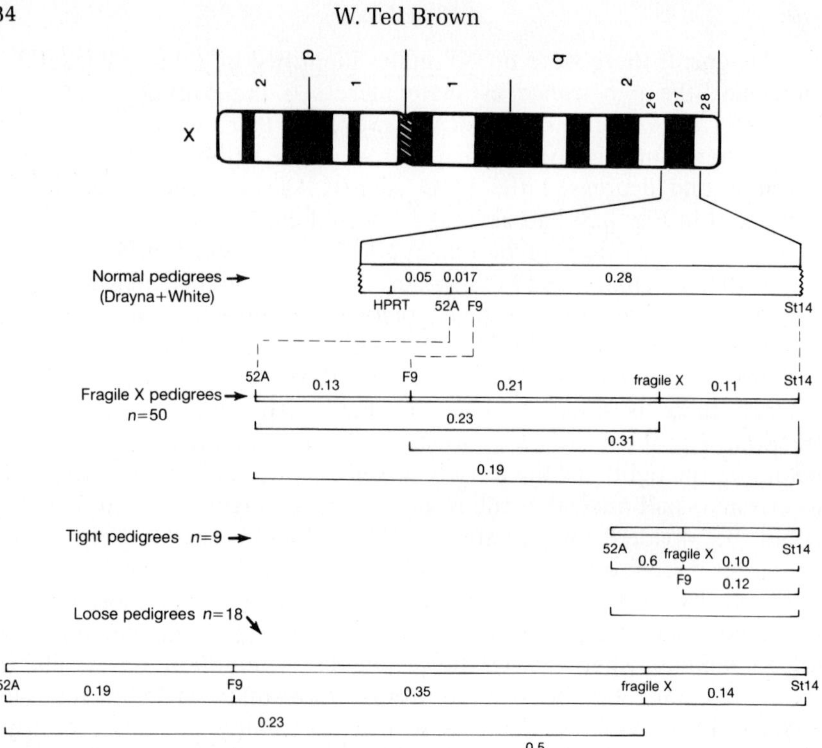

Fig. 4.5. Recombination fractions around the fragile X locus for DNA probes 52A, F9, and fragile X. The data on normal pedigrees are from Drayna and White (1985), and for the fragile X families from Brown *et al.* (1987*b*).

program (Lathrop and Lalouel 1984). The best order and estimated recombinant distances are shown in Fig. 4.6.

The Admixture heterogeneity test was used to determine if there was significant genetic heterogeneity between F9 and fragile X in the 147 families as a whole. The likelihood that families showed overall homogeneous linkage between F9 and fragile X was compared to the likelihood that there were two classes of families; one that showed that tight linkage between F9–fragile X and a second that showed loose linkage. Heterogeneity was found to be the most likely situation at $P<0.0005$. About 20 per cent showed tight F9–fragile X linkage. The families were divided into two groups based upon the F9–fragile X linkage, and multipoint analysis was conducted separately. These results are also shown in Fig. 4.6.

It appeared in our studies that families with a low rate of recombination between F9 and fragile X also showed lower rates of recombination between 52A and F9 as compared to families that showed a high rate of

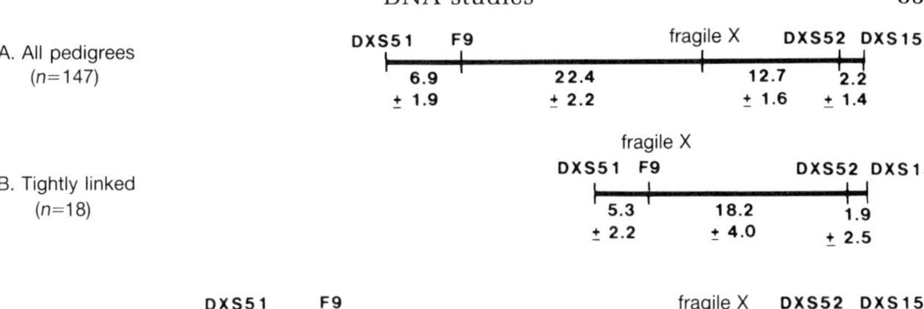

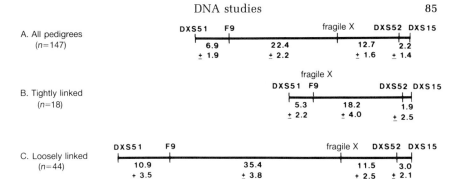

Fig. 4.6. Recombinant fractions for loci around fragile X based on multipoint mapping of 147 fragile X families (Brown *et al.* 1988*a*). Families could be divided into two types based on linkage patterns to F9 which showed significant linkage heterogeneity.

F9–fragile X recombination. But this result was strongly influenced by one particular family, that described by Veenema *et al.* (1987) which had originally been reported by Davies *et al.* (1985). In one branch of this family there were four out of nine individuals with recombination between 52A and F9. However, if the typing of one individual in this family was incorrect and if his result was deleted there would have been 0 out of eight recombinants needed. The particular individual was tested twice in two different labs (Veenema, pers. comm.) and, thus, the result appeared to be correct. This family suggests that there may be a specific hot spot for recombination between 52A and F9 in some families. Data on normal families is needed as it could be that linkage heterogeneity is common and unrelated to fragile X. However, studies of the CEPH panel of families by Thibodeau *et al.* (1988) have so far indicated there is no significant variation in 52A–F9 recombination in normal families.

We localized a set of nine anonymous probes relative to F9, HPRT, and fragile X in 45 fragile X families (Brown *et al.* 1988*b*). Probe 4D-8 which detects a Msp I RFLP at locus DXS98, was known to be unlinked to HPRT (Boggs and Nussbaum 1984). We found it to be closely linked to fragile X (Brown *et al.* 1987*c*). Among 45 fragile X families analysed for linkage, six were informative for the inheritance of 4D-8. They exhibited a peak LOD score of 4.3 at 7 per cent recombination between 4D-8 and fragile X. No evidence for genetic heterogeneity for 4D-8–fragile X was seen using statistical tests, but the number of doubly informative meioses was limited. The families that showed tight F9–fragile X linkage showed no recombinants for 4D-8–fragile X.

A set of random X probes were isolated by Hofker *et al.* (1987). One of these probes cX55.7 (DXS105) was found to be within the region F9–

fragile X by Carpenter *et al.* 1987 and Veenema *et al.* 1987. These findings also were confirmed by Mulley *et al.* (1987). An RFLP for a new probe which appears to be contiguous to cX55.7 was identified by Arveiler *et al.* 1988. This probe, cX33.2, is heterozygous in approximately 44 per cent of women. Use of this probe combined with the previous information on cX55.7 creates a four-allele haplotype which should increase the overall heterozygosity of this locus to nearly 70 per cent.

Carpenter, Thibodeau, and Brown collaborated to establish the relative positions of 4D-8 (DXS98) and cX55.7 (DXS105) among 30 doubly informative families. 4D-8 was found to lie between cX55.7 and fragile X as illustrated in Fig. 4.7. Combining data from the families informative for the three probes, and data of Mulley *et al.* (1988), the best approximate distances between the adjacent probes are illustrated in Fig. 4.8. The probability that a given carrier mother is heterozygous for the probes is also illustrated.

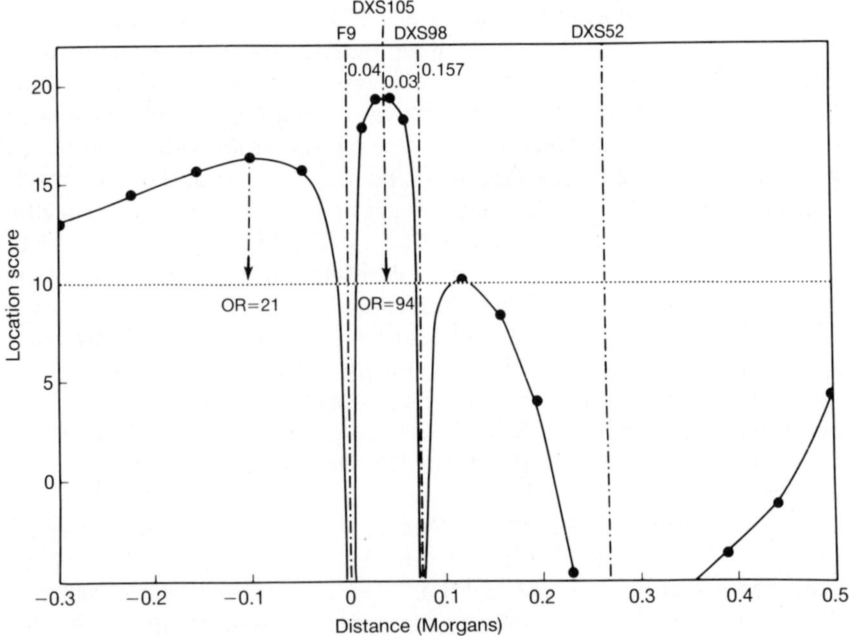

Fig. 4.7. Localization of DXS105 (probe cX55.7) relative to DXS98 (probe 4D-8), F9, and DXS52 (probe ST14) in 30 families using LINKMAP (Carpenter, Thibodeau, and Brown, unpublished). DXS105 was most likely more proximal and further away from DXS52, and therefore from fragile X, than DXS98.

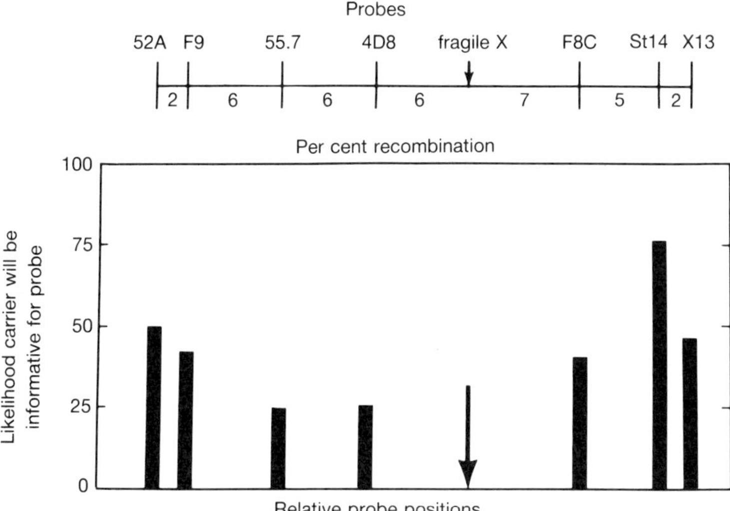

Fig. 4.8. Relative probe positions and usefulness of probes for carrier detection in fragile X. The probes are placed in their approximate best positions (based on Brown *et al.* 1987*b*; Mulley *et al.* 1988; and unpublished results). The position of F8C is assumed to be closer to fragile X than distal probes St14 and X13 (HGM9). However, the positions of st14 and F8C relative to the fragile X remain somewhat uncertain. The likelihood of the various probes being found to be heterozygous in a given carrier is shown below. From this it is seen that about 75 per cent of women are informative for F9 and 52A taken together, and for St14 alone. A new RFLP for cX33.2 (Arveiler *et al.* 1988) should make locus DXS105 informative in the majority of women.

Uses of DNA probes in clinical testing

A common question in the clinical setting, as illustrated in Fig. 4.9, is 'What is the probability of a sister of an affected male being a carrier?' The prior risk of the sister of an affected male being a carrier is 50 per cent, since she has a 50:50 chance of inheriting the fragile X chromosome from her carrier mother. Based upon the studies of Sherman *et al.* (1984, 1985) if the sister is mentally unimpaired, she is less likely to be a carrier and her risks are reduced to approximately 40 per cent. If she is both mentally unimpaired and negative on cytogenetic testing, her risks are reduced to approximately 30 per cent. DNA marker analysis can usually improve these risk estimates. Provided the sister has a different allele or set of alleles than that of her affected sib, her risks can be reduced. Using the estimates of the average recombinant distances to probes on either side of fragile X, shown in Fig. 4.9, and the risk analysis program of LINKAGE (Lathrop and Lalouel 1984), we have calculated

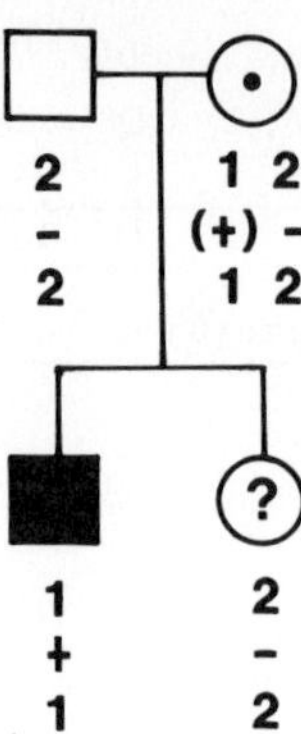

Fig. 4.9. A frequent clinical question: 'What is the likelihood of the sister of an affected male being a carrier?' is illustrated. If adjacent alleles on either side of the fragile X locus are different in the sister than the brother her risks are greatly reduced. Depending on the loci that are informative, as indicated in Table 4.1, her risk may be as low as <0.9 per cent while if two affected brothers are available it may be as low as 0.3 per cent (from Table 4.2).

the risk for the various probes taken singly and as pairs on either side, as shown in Table 4.1. From this table, for example, it can be seen that if a carrier mother is heterozygous for the closest probes 4D-8 and F8, and if the sister has allele types that are different from that of her brother, the risks of the sister being a carrier are reduced from 30 per cent to 0.9 per cent. If two affected sibs are available for testing, then the likelihood of a recombination in both sibs is reduced and the risk calculations are more reliable, as shown in Table 4.2. For example, if a sister has different markers for F8 and 4D-8 than that of two affected brothers, the risks of her being a carrier are reduced to 0.3 per cent. We have found this method of risk analysis using LINKAGE to be of considerable use for genetic counselling (Brown *et al.* 1987*a*). We can assume the average recombinant values are most appropriate for small families. For large

Table 4.1 Carrier risk (one affected sib)

	Proximal probes				
Distal	4D-8	55.7	F9	52A	
F8C	0.9	1.8	2.8	3.1	6.2
St14	1.5	3.2	4.8	5.3	10.6
DX13	1.8	3.7	5.6	6.2	12.3
	5.4	10.6	15.6	17.2	

Table 4.2 Carrier risk (two affected sibs)

Distal	Proximal probes 4D-8	55.7	F9	52A	
F8C	0.3	0.6	1.0	1.1	3.5
St14	0.5	1.1	1.8	2.1	6.4
DX13	0.6	1.3	2.2	2.5	7.8
	3.0	6.4	10.5	12.0	

families, it may be possible to classify them according to F9–fragile X linkage type and use the values shown in Fig. 4.6.

Hypotheses regarding the fragile X mutation

The finding of linkage heterogeneity suggests several alternative explanations. One possibility is a variation in the position of the fragile site relative to the adjacent loci. However, the evidence indicates there are altered rates of recombination between fragile X and the proximal locus F9, but not with distal loci such as DXS52 and DXS15. Another possibility is that the variation in rates of recombination may be based upon structural rearrangements of the nearby chromosomal regions. We originally suggested that an inhibition of recombination due to an inversion might explain our data (Brown *et al.* 1985). There are known inversions in the mammalian genome which alter recombination rates. There are at least two major inverted regions in the *t* complex on mouse chromosome 17, one in the proximal portion and a second in the distal portion. These inverted regions have been shown to lead to deletions and duplications following recombination (Bucan *et al.* 1987). If inversions are present in the human fragile X region, they may alter recombination rates and may result in duplications or deletions which could affect nearby gene expression.

There may be an increase in recombination because of variation in copy number of a sequence that promotes recombination. Pembrey *et al.* 1985 hypothesized that a premutation exists in transmitting males which undergoes meiotic recombination with a recombination 'enhancing sequence' on one of the two homologous female X chromsomes during oogenesis, producing a definitive mutation. The nature of this enhancing sequence of the normal female X chromosome was unidentified. It appeared to us that predictions of this hypothesis were inconsistent with the existing data, since only half of a transmitting male's daughters would receive the wife's enhancing sequence and be at risk for having sons with fragile X expression, whereas all the daughters are apparently at risk. Subsequently, Winter and Pembrey (1986) modified their hypothesis, leaving out the idea that a special enhancing sequence was present, but suggesting that a premutation segregates in the branches of families with transmitting males, while a definitive mutation segregates in branches of families with no evidence for transmitting males. We believe that their modified hypothesis is inconsistent with our data (Brown *et al.* 1987*d*), but they disagree (Winter and Pembrey 1987). A molecular understanding of the underlying sequence variation in the fragile X syndrome should lead to a definitive explanation for the linkage heterogeneity.

Nussbaum *et al.* (1986) suggested that the fragile X region involves a long pyrimidine-rich DNA sequence, such as that proposed by Sutherland (1985) which is prone to undergo unequal crossing-over. We have illustrated this mechanism in Fig. 4.10. A transmitting male could have affected or unaffected non-penetrant male grandsons depending on whether unequal crossing-over occurred in his transmitting female daughters, as illustrated in Fig. 4.11. Unequal crossing-over has been shown to occur in a region of the X chromosome adjacent to fragile X. Studies of the genes encoding red and green visual pigments have shown inherited variations in copy number as a result of unequal recombination (Nathans *et al.* 1986). The green pigment genes show one, two, or three copies which are common alleles in the human genome. Also, studies of the murine X chromosome have shown that unequal crossing-over occurs at a high frequency in the pseudoautosomal region (Harbers *et al.* 1986). There unequal crossing-over appears to be due to the presence of a sequence which is tandemly repeated and highly variable.

Remarkable variations in recombination rates have been found in different genetic strains of mice. For example, Steinmetz *et al.* (1986) have shown there are hot spots for recombination in the mouse major histocompatibility locus which are haplotype dependent. Mouse strain BIO.MOL-SGR showed a 100-fold higher rate of recombination between K and I region marker loci than two other common laboratory mice strains. Sequence data suggest that a genetic element is present in this region which may specifically enhance recombination and which has some homology to the human hypervariable mini-satellite sequence (Jeffreys *et al.* 1985).

Most recombination presumably occurs during meiosis. However, recombination can also occur during mitosis, producing visible events such as sister chromatid exchanges (SCE). Unequal SCEs, could result in duplication or deletion of particular genes. Such a mechanism has been shown to be involved in the magnification of ribosomal RNA genes in *Drosophila* (Tartof 1974). Studies by Weinreb *et al.* (1988) have

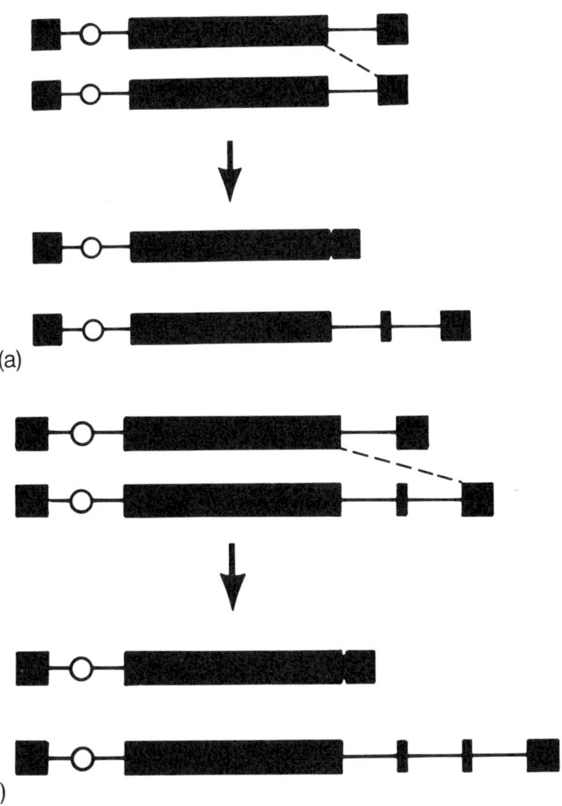

Fig. 4.10. Possible mechanism of unequal crossing-over. Two normal X chromosomes are indicated (a). Following unequal crossing-over, a chromosome with an increased probabilty of further unequal crossing-over is generated (b). Thus a normal X chromosome may evolve to a transmitting non-penetrant X chromosome or to one that is likely to be found in an affected fragile X male.

indicated that unequal SCE has occurred at the immunoglobulin heavy-chain locus in the mouse myeloma cell line MPC II. The heavy-chain constant region gene has been duplicated in a tandem array on the expressed chromosome of the cell line via an unequal sister chromatid exchange. This results in the presence of a germ-line and a non-germ-line form of the gene, which can be detected by variations on genomic Southern blot analysis. Mutagenized derivatives of this cell line have been identified that have amplified the non-germ-line gene form from five- to ten-fold. Other lines have also been found that have deleted the non-germ-line form. Weinreb *et al.* noted that a DNA sequence in this region has the characteristics of zDNA which may be involved in

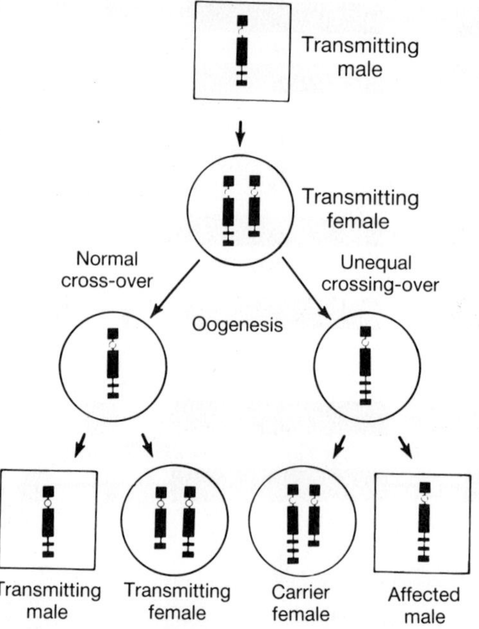

Fig. 4.11. Possible mechanism of transmission of an X chromosome from a transmitting grandfather. Either affected males and carrier females or transmitting males and females may result, depending on whether unequal crossing-over occurs during oogenesis.

promoting recombination and may represent a hot spot for recombination. A similar type of zDNA sequence could be involved in promoting recombination in the human fragile X region.

We have observed a low frequency of apparent fragile-site expression in normal males of approximately 0.5 per cent, and have suggested that a common fragile site may be present at Xq27 in some individuals (Jenkins *et al.* 1986). Perhaps it is only seen at high frequencies when a rearrangement or unequal crossing-over occurs to increase its length and probability of expression. Ledbetter *et al.* 1986 observed that transmitting males could be induced to express a fragile site at Xq27 at a level of approximately 12 per cent when their X chromosomes were analysed in a somatic cell hybrid system. Normal males could also be induced to express a fragile site at a frequency of 5 per cent. Chimpanzee X chromosomes could be induced to show a fragile site at a level of approximately 1 per cent. The elements of the fragile X site expression may be present normally but not expressed except under unusual conditions, such as in this somatic cell hybrid system.

Laird has proposed a novel hypothesis about inheritance of fragile X based upon DNA methylation. He suggests that fragile X results from a mutation that blocks the complete reactivation of an inactivated X chromosome. The original inactivation event normally occurs in females as part of the process of dosage compensation for having two X chromosomes. He proposes that the fragile X syndrome results from the continued transcriptional inactivity of a gene or genes at Xq27 because of a local block to the reactivation which normally occurs prior to oogenesis (Laird 1987; Laird *et al.* 1987). Fragile X chromosomes may be distinguished as either 'mutated' which is an X chromosome which has the potential to block reactivation at Xq27 of a previously inactivated X chromosome, or 'imprinted' which is a mutated fragile X chromosome that has been through a cycle of inactivation and incomplete reactivation. DNA methylation is presumed to be involved in X inactivation. The nature of the underlying sequence variation or mutation is undefined still. A large-scale sequence alteration could be the basis for altered patterns of methylation. Laird has also suggested that it may represent a methylation mutation and not require sequence variation. This hypothesis has many attractive features, and it predicts the altered ratio of affected to unaffected offspring with surprising accuracy. As originally proposed, the theory did not appear to explain the altered segregation ratios which may be seen among the offspring of the mothers of transmitting males (TMs) compared to the offspring of the daughters of TMs, the so-called 'Sherman Paradox' (Turner *et al.* 1986). Laird (1988) has suggested that the ovary from which the stem cells for eggs are derived is mosaic in nature and that the female carrier whose ovary had been populated by stem cells in which more than 50 per cent of the cells had inactivated a fragile X chromosome would have a frequency of chromosome imprinting correspondingly greater than 50 per cent. He has suggested the stem-cell pool-size in the ovary from which the fragile X chromosome containing oocytes are derived, may be as small as two. This leads to the idea the ratios of affected males born to a carrier mother could vary quite markedly and appears to be able to explain the 'Sherman Paradox'.

Although there is little evidence so far to suggest the involvement of methylation differences in comparing fragile X to normal X chromosomes, it is clear that DNA methylation and gene imprinting may be important factors which influence gene expression. For example, Swain *et al.* (1987) reported that a gene (*myc*) introduced into a transgenic mouse only showed expression when the offspring had inherited it from a father. This was correlated with DNA methylation patterns in that the paternally transmitted gene was less methylated than one which was maternally transmitted. Reik *et al.* (1987) studied genomic imprinting of transgenic loci in mice and found a locus which if derived from the father was undermethylated, but if derived from the mother was highly methylated. The methylation pattern was reversed following transmission through an offspring of opposite sex. These studies provide evidence that heritable molecular differences between maternally and paternally derived alleles are imprinted on mouse chromosomes. Direct molecular analysis of the fragile X mutation is needed to determine if a process of DNA methylation and resulting imprinting are involved in the fragile X mutation.

Approaches toward characterizing the fragile X DNA sequence

Rapid progress is being made toward the characterization of adjacent sequences to the fragile X locus and in identifying and characterizing the nature of the mutation. One approach that is becoming technically possible is to employ long-range restriction mapping using infrequent cutter enzymes and to analyse the resulting patterns by the use of pulse field gel electrophoresis (PFGE). Detailed physical mapping of the region around St14 and DX13 by Patterson *et al.* (1987*a*) have employed PFGE. They showed that these probes, and a new probe MN12, were linked within a region of 470 kb. Partial *Mlu* I digests suggested that St14 and DX13 could be as close as 60 kb. In the human genome overall, about 1 centiMorgan (cM) corresponds to approximately 1000 kb, but this data suggests that in this area 1 cM may correspond to a little as 30 kb. Thus, there appears to be a disproportionately high rate of recombination in the region adjacent and proximal to fragile X. Patterson *et al.* (1987*b*) have also shown PFGE evidence for direct linkage of 4D-8(DXS98), cX55.7(DXS105), and cX33.2(DXS152 or DXS105) on the proximal region to fragile X, and F8, G6PD, and 767(DXS115) on the distal region.

In comparing fragile X chromosomes from males in two different families, one that showed tight linkage (F22) and one that showed loose linkage (F20), Dobkin and Brown (1988) presented partial *Sfi* I PFGE results as illustrated in Fig. 4.12, indicating the presence of a large deletion or insertion near locus DXS105. Additional experiments from our laboratory now have shown that these observations are repeated consistently in fragile X chromosomes from different members of these two families. Two other families studied have been found to have similar patterns to that of family F20. Preliminary results of partial digestion analysis of the DXS98 locus have shown that this region may also contain a substantial deletion and insertion in fragile X chromosomes.

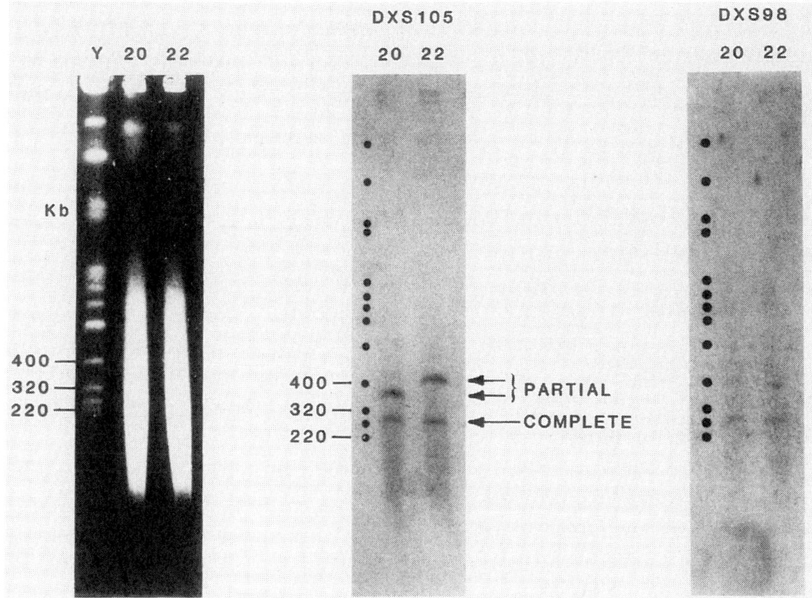

Fig. 4.12. Pulse-field gel electrophoresis of fragile X DNA. DNA from a fragile X male in family 20 (Fig. 4.1) and a fragile X male in family 22 (Fig. 4.2) was partially digested with Sfi I and separated along with yeast chromosome markers (lane Y). The resulting Southern blot was probed to show DXS105 (centre) and DXS98 (right). The first partial and higher-weight secondary partials (which are visbile on this photograph) showed that the chromosomes had a region which differed in size by at least 75 kb, Dobkin and Brown (1988).

Our results suggest that large sequence variations detectable by PFGE may be quite frequent in the fragile X region.

A promising approach to the direct isolation of the fragile X locus is the construction of a somatic cell hybrid containing a translocation of the human fragile X site to a rodent chromosome. Warren *et al.* (1987) isolated several somatic cell hybrids that contained rearranged X chromosomes. DNA-marker studies showed that the rearrangements involved the region at or near to the fragile X site. Fragility at the human X–rodent translocation junction was observed in two hybrid cells but at a lower frequency compared to the intact fragile X chromosome. They suggested that the fragile X region may include a repeated sequence which is prone to recombination. The cloning of these translocation junctions should lead to the isolation of new probes closely linked to fragile X and may allow for characterization of DNA sequences which include the fragile X mutation. Analysis of the mutated region in different non-penetrant and penetrant males should reveal the way the mutation arises. DNA transfer experiments and transgenic animals may show how the mutation affects gene expression and leads to the fragile X syndrome.

Other X-linked non-dysmorphic mental retardation syndromes

While fragile X syndrome appears to account for 30–50 per cent of X-linked mental retardation associated with non-specific or non-dysmorphic features, a number of other individually rare X-linked syndromes are also being studied by linkage. Arveiler *et al.* (1988) studied three such families with about 25 X-linked probes. The first family studied was one initially described by Proops *et al.* (1983), which included six mild to moderately retarded males with large heads, highly arched palates, and testicular volumes in the upper normal to macro-orchid range and for dull or mildly affected females. The males were thought to have the Martin–Bell phenotype. Linkage analysis was most informative for DXS85 (probe 782) with a LOD score maximum of 2.62 at 6 per cent recombination. Thus, the locus for this family was placed at approximately Xp22.2–p22.3 (Fig. 4.13, family A). The second family consisted of eight mild or moderately retarded males in four generations. The phenotype of males in this family included a long face, a prominent jaw, and large ears without macro-orchidism. Linkage analysis included three available males in this family and suggested linkage to locus DXS164 at Xp21.2 (probes pERT87.15 and 87.8) with a LOD score maximum of 1.59 at 0 per cent recombination (Fig. 4.13, family B). The third family included seven moderately retarded males without macro-orchidism or dysmorphic faces. Linkage analysis showed a peak LOD score with locus DXS159 at Xq12–q13 (cpX73) of 2.53 (Fig. 4.13, family D).

A study of Suthers *et al.* (1988) of a large family with eight available moderately retarded non-dysmorphic and non-macro-orchid males showed a peak LOD score of 2.12 with the centromeric marker DXS14 (probe p58.1) (Fig. 4.13, family C). A family with X-linked mental retardation, skeletal anomalies, and normal faces with a broad nasal bridge was studied by Dlouhy *et al.* (1987). Linkage to DXS52 (probe St14-1) gave a peak LOD score of 3.27 at 0 per cent recombination with a most likely localization of this syndrome distal to fragile X (Figure 4.13, family E). These studies have led to the conclusion that there are likely to be a number of distinct non-dysmorphic forms of X-linked metal retardation that map to regions other than the fragile X locus.

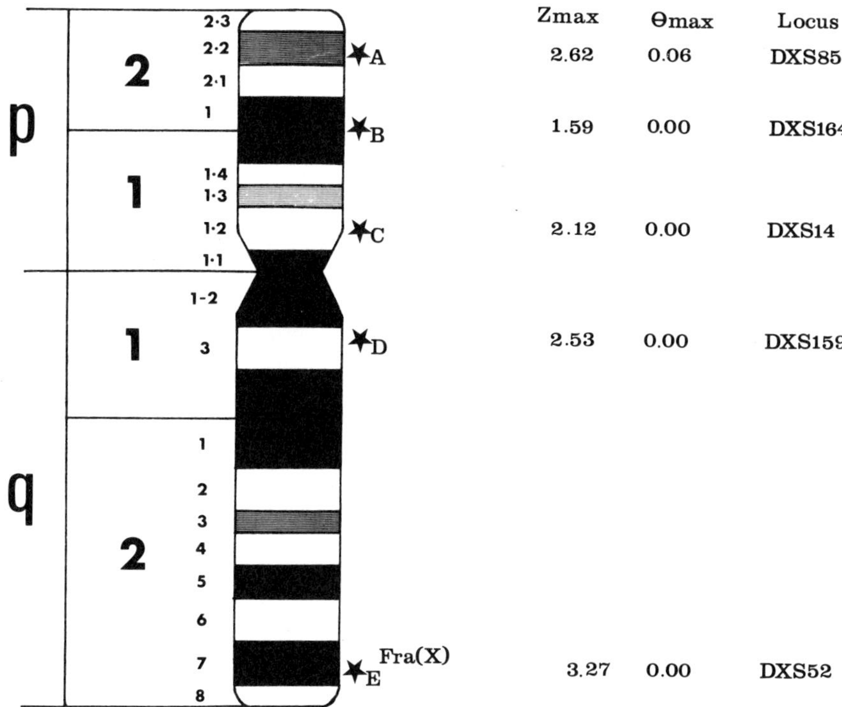

Fig. 4.13. Probable X chromosome locations of non-specific (non-dysmorphic) mental retardation syndromes. Families A, B, and D from Arveiler *et al.* (1988). Family C from Suthers *et al.* (1988). Family E from Dlouhy *et al.* (1983).

References

Arveiler, B., Alembik, Y., Hanauer, A., Jacobs, P., Tranebjaerg, L., Mikkelsen, M., Puissant, H., Larget Piet, L., and Mandel, J. L. (1988). Linkage analysis suggests at least two loci for X-linked non-specific mental retardation. *American Journal of Medical Genetics*, **30**, 473–83.

Arveiler, B., Oberle, I., Vincent, A., Hofker, M. H., Pearson, P. L., and Mandel, J. L. (1988). Genetic mapping of the Xq27-q28 region: new RFLP markers useful for diagnostic applications in fragile X and hemophilia B families. *American Journal of Human Genetics*, **42**, 380–9.

Boggs, B. A. and Nussbaum, R. L. (1984). Two anonymous X-specific human sequences detecting restriction fragment length polymorphisms in region Xq26-qter. *Somatic Cell and Molecular Genetics*, **10**, 607–13.

Brown, W. T., Gross, A. C., Chan, C. B., and Jenkins, E. C. (1985). Genetic linkage heterogeneity in the fragile X syndrome. *Human Genetics*, **71**, 11–18.

Brown, W. T., Gross, A. C., Chan, C. B., and Jenkins, E. C. (1986). DNA linkage studies in the fragile X syndrome suggest genetic heterogeneity. *American Journal of Medical Genetics*, **23**, 643–64.

Brown, W. T. *et al.* (1987*a*). Clinical use of DNA markers in the fragile (X) syndrome for carrier detection and prenatal diagnosis. In *Nucleic acid probes in diagnosis of human genetic diseases*, (ed. A. M. Willey), pp. 11–34. Alan R. Liss, New York.

Brown, W. T. *et al.* (1987*b*). Further evidence for genetic heterogeneity in the fragile X syndrome. *Human Genetics*, **75**, 311–21.

Brown, W. T., Wu, Y., Gross, A. C., Chan, C. B., Dobkin, C. S., and Jenkins, E. C. (1987*c*). RFLP for linkage analysis of fragile X syndrome. *Lancet*, **i**, 280.

Brown, W. T., Sherman, S. L., and Dobkin, C. S. (1987*d*). Hypothesis regarding the nature of the fragile X mutation. A reply to Winter and Pembrey. *Human Genetics*, **75**, 294–305.

Brown, W. T. *et al.* (1988*a*). Multilocus analysis of the fragile X syndrome. *Human Genetics*, **78**, 201–5.

Brown, W. T., Wu, Y., Gross, A. C., Chan, C. B., Dobkin, C. S., and Jenkins, E. C. (1988*b*). Multipoint linkage of 9 Anonymous Probes to HPRT, Factor 9, and Fragile X. *American Journal of Medical Genetics*, **30**, 551–66.

Bucan, M. *et al.* (1987). Deletion and duplication of DNA sequences is associated with the embryonic lethal phenotype of the t^9 complementation group of the mouse t complex. *Genes and Development*, **1**, 376–85.

Camerino, G., Mattei, M. G., Mattei, J. F., Jaye, M., and Mandel, J. L. (1983). Close linkage of fragile X linked mental retardation syndrome to haemophilia B and transmission through a normal male. *Nature*, **306**, 701–7.

Carpenter, N. J., Veenema, H., Bakker, E., Hofker, M. H., and Pearson, P. L. (1987). A new DNA probe proximal to and closely linked to fragile X. *American Journal of Medical Genetics*, **27**, 731–32.

Choo, K. H. *et al.* (1984). Linkage analysis of X-linked mental retardation with and without fragile-X using factor IX gene probe. *Lancet*, **i**, 349.

Connor, J. M., Pirritt, L. A., Yates, J. R. W., Crossley, J. A., Imrie, S. J., and Colgan, J. M. (1987). Linkage analysis using multiple Xq DNA polymorphisms in normal families, families with the fragile X syndrome and other families with X-linked conditions. *Journal of Medical Genetics*, **24**, 14–22.

Davies, K. E., *et al.* (1985). Linkage studies of X-linked mental retardation: High frequency of recombination in the telomeric region of the human X chromosome. *Human Genetics*, **70**, 249–55.

Dlouhy, S. R., Christian, J. C., Haines, J. L., Conneally, P. M., and Hodes, M. E. (1987). Localization of the gene for a syndrome of X-linked skeletal dysplasia and mental retardation to Xq27-qter. *Human Genetics*, **75**, 136–9.

Dobkin, C. S., and Brown, W. T. (1988). Pulsed-field gradient-gel studies around the fragile site. *American Journal of Medical Genetics*, **30**, 593–600.

Drayna, D. and White, R. (1985). The genetic linkage map of the human X chromosome. *Science*, **230**, 753–8.

Forster-Gibson, C. J., Mulligan, L. M., Partington, M. W., Simpson, N. E., Holden, J. J. A., and White, B. N. (1985). The genetic distance between the coagulation factor IX gene and the locus for the fragile-X syndrome: clinical implications. *Journal of Neurogenetics*, **2**, 231–7.

Forster-Gibson, C. J., Mulligan, L. M., Simpson, N. E., White, B. N., and Holden, J. J. A. (1986). An assessment of the use of flanking DNA markers for fra(X) syndrome carrier detection and prenatal diagnosis. *American Journal of Medical Genetics*, **23**, 665–83.

Harbers, K., Soriano, P., Muller, U., and Jaenisch, R. (1986). High frequency of unequal recombination in pseudoautosomal region shown by proviral insertion in transgenic mouse. *Nature*, **324**, 682–5.

Hofker, M. H. *et al.* (1987). Efficient isolation of H chromosome-specific single-copy probes from a cosmid library of a human X/hamster hybrid cell line: Mapping of new probes close to the locus for X-linked mental retardation. *American Journal of Human Genetics*, **40**, 312–28.

Giannelli, F., Morris, A. H., Garrett, C., Daker, M., Thurston, C., and Smith, C. A. B. (1987). Genetic heterogeneity of X-linked mental retardation with fragile X. Association of tight linkage to factor IX and incomplete penetrance in males. *Annals of Human Genetics*, **51**, 107–24.

Goonewardena, P. *et al.* (1986). Analysis of fragile X-mental retardation families using flanking polymorphic DNA probes. *Clinical Genetics*, **30**, 249–54.

Jeffreys, A. J., Wilson, V., and Thein, S. L. (1985). Hypervariable minisatellite regions in human DNA. *Nature*, **314**, 67–73.

Jenkins, E. C. *et al.* (1986). Low frequencies of apparently fragile X chromosomes in normal cultures: a possible explanation. *Experimental Cell Biology*, **54**, 40–8.

Laird, C. D. (1987). Proposed mechanism of inheritance and expression of the human fragile X-syndrome of mental retardation. *Genetics*, **117**, 587–99.

Laird, C. D., Jaffe, E., Karpen, G., Lamb, M., and Nelson, R. (1987). Fragile sites in human chromosomes as regions of late-replicating DNA. *Trends in Genetics*, **3**, (10), 274–81.

Laird, C. D. (1988). Fragile X mutations proposed to block complete reactivation in females of an inactive X chromosome. *American Journal of Medical Genetics*, **30**, 693–6.

Landoulsi, A., deBlois, M. C., Guérin, P., Rethoré, M. O., Lejeune, J., and Lucotte, G. (1985). Recombinaison entre le site fragile Xq27 et le gène du facteur IX de la coagulation. *Annales de Génétique*, **28**, (4), 201–5.

Lathrop, G. M. and Lalouel, J. M. (1984). Easy calculations of lod scores and genetic risks on small computers. *American Journal of Human Genetics*, **36**, 460–5.

Ledbetter, D. H., Ledbetter, S. A., and Nussbaum, R. L. (1986). Implications of fragile X expression in normal males for the nature of the mutation. *Nature*, **324**, 161–3.

Mulley, J. C., Geden, A. K., Thorn, K. A., Bates, L. J., and Sutherland, G. R. (1987). Linkage and genetic counseling for the fragile X using DNA probes 52A, F9, DX13, and St14. *American Journal of Medical Genetics*, **27**, 435–49.

Mulley, J., Turner, G., Bain, S., and Sutherland, G. R. (1988). Linkage between the fragile X and F9, DXS52 (ST14), DXS98 (4D-8) and DXS105 (cX55.7). *American Journal of Medical Genetics*, **30**, 567–80.

Mulligan, L. M., *et al.* (1985). Genetic mapping of DNA segments relative to the locus for the fragile X syndrome at Xq27.3. *American Journal of Human Genetics*, **37**, 463–72.

Nathans, J., Piantanida, T. P., Eddy, R. L., Shows, T. B., and Hogness, D. S. (1986). Molecular genetics of inherited variation in human color vision. *Science*, **232**, 203–10.

Nussbaum, R. L., Airhart, S. D., and Ledbetter, D. H. (1986). Recombination and amplification of pyrimidine-rich sequences may be responsible for initiation and progression of the Xq27 fragile site: an hypothesis. *American Journal of Medical Genetics*, **23**, 715–21.

Oberle, I., Drayna, D., Camerino, G., Kloepfer, C., and Mandel, J. L. (1985*a*). The telomeric region of the human X chromosome long arm: presence of a highly polymorphic DNA marker and analysis of recombination frequency. *Proceedings of the National Academy of Sciences USA*, **82**, 2824–8.

Oberle, I., Mandel, J. L., Boue, J., Mattei, M. G., and Mattei, J. F. (1985*b*). Polymorphic DNA markers in prenatal diagnosis of fragile X syndrome. *Lancet*, **i**, 871.

Oberle, I. *et al.* (1986). Genetic analysis of the fragile-X mental retardation syndrome with two flanking polymorphic DNA markers. *Proceedings of the National Academy of Sciences USA*, **83**, 1016–20.

Oberle, I. *et al.* (1987). Multipoint genetic mapping of the Xq26-q28 region in families with fragile X mental retardation and in normal families reveals tight linkage of markers in q26-q27. *Human Genetics*, **77**, 60–5.

Ott, J. (1985). Analysis of human genetic linkage. Johns Hopkins University Press, Baltimore.

Patterson, M. *et al.* (1987*a*). Mapping of DNA markers close to the fragile site on the human X chromosome at Xq27.3. *Nucleic Acids Research*, **15**, (6), 2639–51.

Patterson, M. *et al.* (1987*b*). Physical mapping studies on the human X chromosome in the region X127-Xqter. *Genomics*, **1**, 297–306.

Pembrey, M. E., Winter, R. M., and Davies, K. E. (1985). A premutation that generates a defect at crossing over explains the inheritance of fragile X mental retardation. *American Journal of Medical Genetics*, **21**, 709–17.

Proops, R., Mayer, M., and Jacobs, P. A. (1983). A study of mental retardation in children in the island of Hawaii. *Clinical Genetics*, **23**, 81–96.

Reik, W., Collick, A., Norris, M. L., Barton, S. C., and Surani, M. A. (1987). Genomic imprinting determines methylation of parental alleles in transgenic mice. *Nature*, **328**, 248–54.

Risch, N. (1988). A new statistical test for linkage heterogeneity. *American Journal of Human Genetics*, **42**, 353–64.

Sherman, S. L., Morton, N. E., Jacobs, P. A., and Turner, G. (1984). The marker (X) syndrome: a cytogenetic and genetic analysis. *Annals of Human Genetics*, **48**, 21–37.

Sherman, S. L. *et al.* (1985). Further segregation analysis of the fragile X syndrome with special reference to transmitting males. *Human Genetics*, **69**, 289–99.

Steinmetz, M., Stephen, D., and Lindahl, K. F. (1986). Gene organization and recombinational hotspots in the murine major histocompatibility complex. *Cell*, **44**, 895–904.

Sutherland, G. R., Baker, E., and Fratinia, A. (1985). Excess thymidine induces folate sensitive fragile sites. *American Journal of Medical Genetics*, **22**, 433–43.

Suthers, G. K., Turner, G., and Mulley, J. C. (1988). A non-syndromal form of X-linked mental retardation (XLMR) is linked to *DXS14*. *American Journal of Medical Genetics*, **30**, 485–91.

Swain, J. L., Stewart, T. A., and Leder, P. (1987). Parental legacy determines methylation and expression of an autosomal transgene: a molecular mechanism for parental imprinting. *Cell*, **50**, 719–27.

Tartof, K. (1974). Unequal miotic sister chromatid exchange as the mechanism of ribosomal RNA gene magnification. *Proceedings of the National Academy of Sciences USA*, **71**, 1272–6.

Thibodeau, S. N. *et al.* (1988). Linkage analysis using multiple DNA polymorphic markers in normal families and in families with fragile X syndrome. *Human Genetics*, **79**, 219–27.

Turner, G. *et al.* (1986). Conference report: Second International Workshop on the Fragile X and on X-linked Mental Retardation. *American Journal of Medical Genetics*, **23**, 11–67.

Veenema, H., Carpenter, N. J., Bakker, E., Hofker, M. H., Ward, A. M., and Pearson, P. L. (1987). The fragile X syndrome in a large family III. Investigations on linkage of flanking DNA markers with the fragile site Xq27. *Journal of Medical Genetics*, **24**, 413–21.

Warren, S. T., Glover, T. W., Davidson, R. L. and Jagadeeswaran, P. (1985). Linkage and recombination between fragile X-linked mental retardation and the factor IX gene. *Human Genetics*, **69**, 44–6.

Warren, S. T., Zhang, F., Licameli, G. R., and Peters, J. F. (1987). The fragile X site in somatic cell hybrids: an approach for molecular cloning of fragile sites. *Science*, **237**, 420–3.

Weinreb, A., Katzenberg, D. R., Gilmore, G. L., and Birshtein, B. K. (1988). Site of unequal sister chromatid exchange contains a potential Z-DNA-forming tract. *Proceedings of the National Academy of Sciences USA*, **85**, 529–33.

Winter, R. M. and Pembrey, M. E. (1986). Analysis of linkage relationships between genetic markers around the fragile X locus with special reference to the daughters of normal transmitting males. *Human Genetics*, **74**, 93–7.

Winter, R. and Pembrey, M. (1987). Interpretation of the heterogeneity in the linkage relationships of DNA markers around the fragile X locus. *Human Genetics*, **77**, 297–8.

Zoll, B. *et al.* (1985). Evidence against close linkage of the loci for fraXq of Martin–Bell syndrome and for factor IX. *Human Genetics*, **71**, 122–6.

5 Cytogenetics of the fragile site at Xq27

NIELS TOMMERUP

Introduction

The chromosomal fragile site at Xq27—fragile X—was first described by Lubs in 1969 and later in other families with X-linked mental retardation (Escalanté *et al.* 1971; Giraud *et al.* 1976; Harvey *et al.* 1977). In 1981, Richards *et al.* found the fragile X in affected individuals from a family with X-linked mental retardation which was originally described by Martin and Bell in 1943, and the term Martin–Bell syndrome (MB) has since been used as a synonym for the fragile X syndrome.

Few phenomena have had such an impact on cytogenetics as the fragile X. MB is second only to Down syndrome as a specific cause of mental retardation, and since it is heritable, each proband leads to analysis of an often extensive number of relatives. Only a fraction of the cells will express the fragile X in a positive individual, and only when specific culturing conditions are met. An increased number of cultures and the necessity to screen a large number of cells from each individual are technical factors which put a heavy load on the cytogenetic laboratory.

Morphology and detection

The fragile site at Xq is positioned in sub-band Xq27.3 as judged from high resolution G- and R-band studies (Brookwell and Turner 1983; Krawczun *et al.* 1985), and by scanning transmission electron microscopy (Harrison *et al.* 1983). Like other fragile sites, the fragile X is a non-staining gap of varying size, often involving both chromatids, and always with the same position on the specific chromosome (Sutherland 1979*a*). Expression increases in prometaphase chromosomes (Barbi and Steinbach 1982). Acentric fragments are occasionally seen in association with expression of the fragile X (Tuckerman *et al.* 1986). Deletion at Xq27 in 2–4 per cent of the cells may occur (Fitchett and Seabright 1984; Tuckerman *et al.* 1986) although others have failed to detect this (Jalbert *et al.* 1983). Triradial figures, due to mitotic non-disjunction of the distal fragment (Ford and Madan 1973; Ferguson-Smith 1977; Noel *et al.* 1977; Tommerup 1987*a*), are found in approximately 1–2.5 per cent of the fragile X positive metaphases (Jenkins *et al.* 1986*c*; Tommerup 1987*a*).

The presence of the fragile X is evident in the majority of expressing cells. However, the morphology of the distal fragment may vary and, in some cells, uncertainty may exist whether the fragile site is expressed or not (Fig. 5.1).

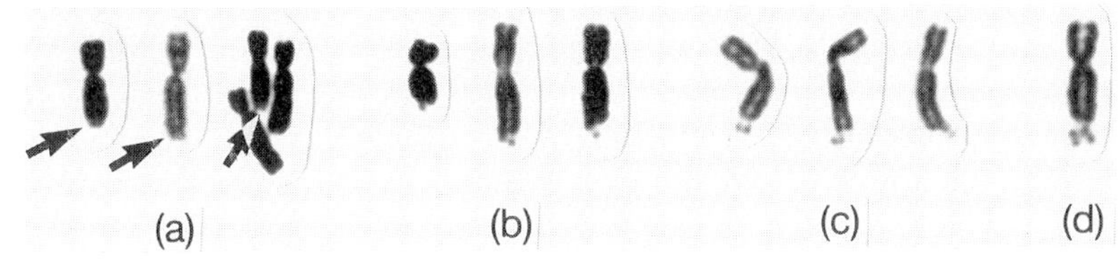

Fig. 5.1. Variable morphology of the fragile site at Xq27. In (a) the terminal part of Xq is somewhat tapered (arrows), but these chromosomes would not be considered to express the fragile site. (b) Fragility of one chromatid; (c) fragility of both chromatids; (d) triradial figure. Giemsa staining following identification with quinacrine.

Telomeric lesions on other C-group chromosomes, notably the common fragile site at 6q, may mimic the fragile X in unbanded preparations (Leversha *et al.* 1981; Vekemans *et al.* 1983; Daniel *et al.* 1984*b*), and thus some kind of banding technique is recommended for fragile X screening. One commonly used method is to screen for fragile sites on Giemsa stained, unbanded chromosomes, then destain, band, and relocate the same metaphases to check the identity of the fragile chromosomes (Howard-Peebles 1981; Soudek and McGregor 1981). Trypsin-G banding can be used, especially if the chromosomes are slightly undertrypsinized, to decrease the swelling of the chromosomes. We routinely use Q-banded preparations for fragile X screening since this banding technique is both rapid, reproducible, and does not affect chromosomal morphology. Although the distal fragment is pale on staining with quinacrine, it is easy to see in the microscope, whereas photographic reproduction often is inferior.

Induction methods

Thymidylate deficiency

The first crucial observation of the bizarre behaviour of the fragile X came when Sutherland (1977) found that the expression was affected by the choice of medium used. Folic acid (FA), thymidine, and the thymidine-analogue, bromodeoxyuridine (BrdU), inhibited the expression of the fragile X, whereas the folate antagonist methotrexate (MTX) induced the fragile X (Sutherland 1979*a*). The likely explanation was that incorporation of thymidine into cellular DNA was involved. Further evidence for this came when fluorodeoxyuridine (FdU), a specific inhibitor of thymidylate synthase, was found to be a very effective inducer of the fragile X (Glover 1981; Tommerup *et al.* 1981). FdU is converted by thymidine kinase to FdUMP which is the active agent. As predicted, FdU was an effective inducer in the presence of FA but not in the presence of thymidine (Glover 1981; Brookwell *et al.* 1982; Gardiner *et al.* 1984) since the latter is converted to dTMP by the thymidine kinase salvage pathway which is not affected by FdU. Other inhibitors of thymidylate synthase, trifluorothymidine and fluorodeoxycytidine, are also efficient inducers (Tommerup, in Hecht *et al.* 1982; Jacky and Sutherland 1983). Furthermore, when cultured without the presence of exogeneous thymidine, spontaneous expression was observed in hybrids between fragile X cells and rodent cell lines deficient in thymidylate synthase, when human chromosomes 18 carrying the thymidylate synthase locus were lost (Hori *et al.* 1985; Nussbaum *et al.* 1985).

Trimethoprim and pyrimethamine—inhibitors of dihydrofolate reductase—induce the fragile X (Lejeune *et al.* 1982; Calva-Mercado *et al.* 1983), and such antibiotics should perhaps be used with caution in patients with MB (Hecht and Glover 1983).

In some individuals the presence of methionine in the culture medium is necessary for the induction of the fragile X in folate-deficient medium (Howard-Peebles and Pryor 1981). However, even without the presence of methionine, the fragile X can be induced by FdU (Glover and Howard-Peebles 1983) so the effect of methionine on fragile X expression might be due to an antifolate effect (Reidy 1984; Howard-Peebles 1986).

Although folate and thymidylate metabolisms are involved in the induction of the fragile X, several studies have indicated the presence of normal folate and thymidylate pathways in fragile X patients (Nielsen *et al.* 1983*a*; Popovitch *et al.* 1983; Erbe 1984; Wang and Erbe 1985; Froster-Iskenius *et al.* 1986), suggesting that the nucleotide-pool imbalance behind the expression of the fragile X is unrelated to the biochemical basis of the disease.

Deoxycytidine diphosphate deficiency

A novel mode of fragile X induction was described by Sutherland *et al.* (1985), who found expression of the fragile X in high concentrations of thymidine. Thymidine in mM concentration is an effective inhibitor of

DNA synthesis ('thymidine block'). The elevated pool of dTTP inhibits ribonucleotide reductase, thus inhibiting the reduction of cytidine diphosphate to deoxycytidine diphosphate (Reichard *et al.* 1961). In analogy with this, the induction of the fragile X by excess thymidine was inhibited by deoxycytidine. This finding was of prime importance for two reasons:

(1) any model of the molecular basis of the fragile site should explain that low levels of both dTTP and dCTP will lead to expression; and

(2) it provided an alternative way to induce the fragile X which was not based on dTTP depletion.

Practical aspects of induction in peripheral blood (PBL)

Due to the frequency of MB syndrome, and the difficulty involved in recognizing the condition clinically, especially in children, any chromosome laboratory engaged in diagnosis of the mentally handicapped should use a routine culturing method which will permit the induction of the fragile X.

The various techniques used for fragile X induction all involve inhibition of DNA synthesis; one consequence of this is an improved chromosomal morphology. Although there may be fewer mitoses in such cultures, those left generally have longer, slender chromosomes. So another benefit of using a medium composition suitable for fragile X induction in routine cultures is an improved resolution of banded chromosomes.

The number of cells which should be analysed would ideally depend on the phenotype, position in the pedigree, expression in other affected relatives, and the efficiency of the laboratory in detecting the fragile X, as well as the background frequency in normal individuals (De Arce 1983; Hecht and Sutherland 1984; De Arce *et al.* 1986; Soudek 1986). However, 100 cells have been chosen arbitrarily by many laboratories, and if we also decide that at least two fragile X positive cells are necessary for the diagnosis, carriers with a 4 per cent expression of the fragile X will be diagnosed with a 95 per cent probability (De Arce 1983).

Choice of medium

Induction by thymidylate depletion (FA−, FdU, MTX) requires the absence or very low concentrations of thymidine in the medium. For induction by low folate, Parker TC 199 is the most widely used, due to the low content of FA (0.01 mg/l). Specific folate-free media have also been used, e.g. MEM-FA (Sutherland 1979*a*). The fragile X can efficiently be induced by FdU in folate-rich media (e.g. McCoy's Medium 5A; 10 mg/l) (Tommerup *et al.* 1981).

One of the major advantages with the induction based on excess thymidine will probably be that the media composition is not so critical, since very few media contain deoxycytidine.

Serum

Serum may reduce the expression under folate-deficient conditions due to the presence of FA or thymidine, and should thus be used with only a minimum concentration to ensure a reasonable proliferation. We have, with success, replaced fetal calf serum with the less expensive new-born calf serum (5 per cent). Induction by excess thymidine may have the advantage that it does not matter whether FA or thymidine are present in the serum, so a higher serum content could conceivably be used with this method to increase the mitotic index.

Choice of inhibitor

von Koskull and Nordström (1987) reported that excess thymidine (300 mg/l) was as good or slightly superior than FdU when used for the detection of fragile X in mentally retarded or subnormal males and females, whereas there was no difference between excess thymidine and FdU when applied to normal carrier females. Thus, for induction of the fragile X in lymphocytes, there are probably no inhibitors of choice if the medium and serum content have been selected appropriately. If a specific inhibitor has proven satisfactory and some experience has been gained with this, it is probably wise to continue with this.

Storage/transportation

Storage of peripheral blood (4–7 days), either in the refrigerator or due to transportation, reduces the expression (Jacobs *et al.* 1980; Fonatsch 1981; Mattei *et al.* 1981; Brookwell *et al.* 1982; Fonatsch and Schwinger 1983). In the latter study, FdU was reported to increase the expression in a few blood samples delayed in transit, whereas Soudek (1985) reported that MTX and FdU did not affect this decrease rate. Soudek also observed some individual variability in the decrease rate, and this might explain some conflicting results regarding the effect of storage on fragile X expression (Jacky and Sutherland 1983). Release of thymidine/FA from dying cells would be one possible explanation for a decrease in expression following storage. Another might be reduced proliferation in stored lymphocytes. Whatever the explanation, undue storage and transportation of blood samples for fragile X analysis should be avoided.

Cell density

High cell density during culture was found to reduce the expression in a lymphoblastoid cell line and in PBL from an affected male (Krawczun *et al.* 1986). They suggested that this might be due to decay or utilization of FdU in the high density cultures, permitting the cells to regain normal thymidine synthesis. Cantú *et al.* (1985) showed a decrease of FdU activity over a period of days, and the reduction of activity increased with increasing cell densities. In the study by Krawczun *et al.* (1986), the optimal cell density for expression in both the lymphoblastoid cell line and in PBL was about 0.5×10^5 cells/ml.

Duration of culture

The duration of culture has been reported to affect the expression of the fragile X in PBL (Sutherland 1977; Jacobs *et al.* 1980; Jennings *et al.* 1980; Howard-Peebles and Pryor 1981; Mattei *et al.* 1981). The optimal expression was found in 72- and 96-hour cultures, with inferior expression in 48-hour cultures (Sutherland and Hecht 1985). Induction of the fragile X on BrdU-substituted chromosomes by excess thymidine have shown expression in cells which have undergone both one (M1), two (M2), and three (M3) replication cycles in the presence of BrdU (Tommerup 1986) (Fig. 5.2), indicating that only one replication cycle is necessary for expression.

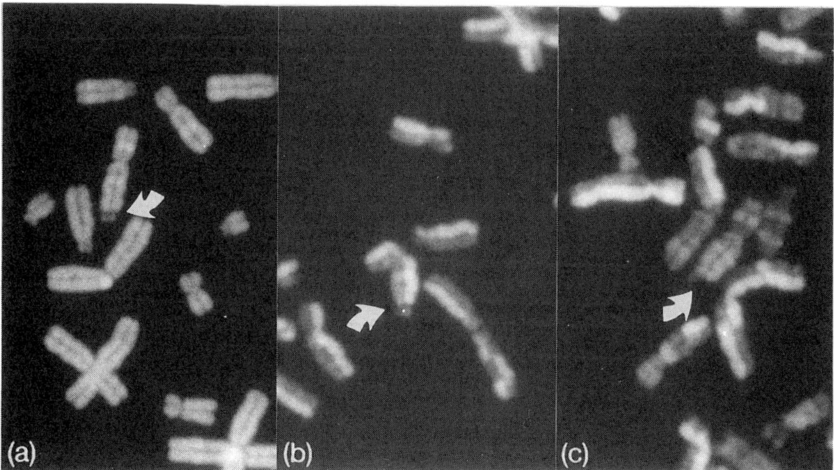

Fig. 5.2. Expression of the fragile site at Xq27 (arrows) in lymphocyte chromosomes following incorporation of BrdU for (a) one (M1), (b) two (M2), and (c) three (M3) replications. Notice the simultaneous banding and the differentially stained sister chromatids in M2 and part of M3 chromosomes. Acridine orange staining.

Treatment with folic acid

Due to the involvement of FA in the expression of the fragile X, the clinical effects of high doses of FA have been tested in a number of patients (Lejeune *et al.* 1981; Hagerman *et al.* 1983, 1986; Brown *et al.* 1984, 1986; Erbe, 1984; Nielsen and Tommerup 1984; Gustavson *et al.* 1985; Froster-Iskenius *et al.* 1986). At the cellular level, the expression of the fragile X is highly reduced during *in vivo* treatment if expression is attempted by growth in folate-deficient medium alone. However, in the presence of FdU, the expression of the fragile X is as high or even higher than before treatment (Nielsen and Tommerup 1984), indicating that expression has only been masked by the high intracellular levels of folate.

Expression in cord blood

Sutherland (1982, 1985) screened a large series of neonates for the presence of folate-sensitive fragile sites, and did not detect the fragile X among 1810 males and 1648 females. Although this was not significantly different from the expected number (one male, two females), the method employed was probably not ideal for this purpose: the cord blood was grown in folate-free medium only, and it is known that the concentration of FA in cord blood is higher than in normal peripheral blood (Matoth *et al.* 1964). Furthermore, pregnant women often receive additional vitamins, including FA, which would further increase the folate level in cord blood. Thus, analysis for the fragile X in cord blood, both after prenatal diagnosis and in population screenings, should include culture(s) with FdU or excess thymidine.

Expression in different cell types

The fragile X has been demonstrated in a number of different cell types, indicating that it is not a cell-specific phenomenon (see Sutherland and Hecht 1985). Expression is found in cell clones (Steinbach *et al.* 1983), indicating that it is not a case of chromosomal mosaicism. The expression is generally highest in PBL, and is often similar whether folate deficiency or inhibitors (FdU, MTX) are used. In contrast, the use of inhibitors are often necessary for expression in other cell types.

Genetic factors affecting expression

Expression in different ethnic groups

The fragile X has been identified in all ethnic groups studied, including Caucasians, Blacks (Howard-Peebles and Stoddard 1980*b*), Indians

(Soysa *et al.* 1982), Orientals (Arinami *et al.* 1986), and Aboriginals (Turner, pers. comm.). Similar prevalence rates (0.7–0.8/1000 among males and 0.4–0.5/1000 among females) were found in an English and a Finnish population (Webb *et al.* 1986; Kähkönen *et al.* 1987), whereas the estimated figures were 0.4 and 0.2/1000 among males and females, respectively, in an Australian population (Turner *et al.* 1986).

Expression in normal males

Although the fragile X was initially stated not to occur in normal males (Soudek and Gorzny 1980), low frequencies of lesions resembling the fragile X have been found in normal control PBL cultures (Proops and Webb 1981; Steinbach *et al.* 1982; Jenkins *et al.* 1986*a*; Ledbetter *et al.* 1986*c*). In the latter study, this frequency could be increased in human/ Chinese hamster hybrid cells, and it was suggested that a common fragile site is present in the region Xq27 in all individuals, and that this common fragile site may be mutated in individuals with the fragile X. Recently, Ledbetter and Ledbetter (1987) reported that high levels of aphidicolin induced an apparently common fragile site in the Xq27 region in both normal and affected males.

Daker *et al.* (1981) reported high expression (15 per cent, 9 per cent) in PBL from two normal brothers without any family history of MB, and G. C. Webb *et al.* (1981) observed a frequency of 26 per cent fragile X in an apparently intellectually normal maternal grandfather of a boy with MB. However, no other phenotypic data were provided in these reports.

Expression in affected males

The degree of expression in affected males varies considerably, from less than 4 per cent to 50 per cent or more (Fig. 5.3). Although rather constant from time to time in the same individual (Eberle *et al.* 1982*b*; Soudek *et al.* 1984; Jenkins *et al.* 1986*d*), a small but significant drop in the expression after the age of 40 has been reported (Turner and Partington 1988). The expression within a family tends to be of the same magnitude, suggesting that this is a genetically determined trait (Brookwell *et al.* 1982; Hecht *et al.* 1986). Also, the degree of expression tends to correlate with the degree of mental impairment in affected males (Chudley *et al.* 1983; Turner and Partington 1988).

Data from monozygous (MZ) male twins and triplets with the fragile X indicates that the expression in PBL is concordant (Gillberg 1983; van der Hagen *et al.* 1983; Rocchi *et al.* 1985; Rosenblatt *et al.* 1985; Tommerup *et al.* 1987*a*), but in the latter study discordant clinical affection, including facial dysmorphism, was noted. Further analysis of twins with the fragile X may be rewarding, especially in the light of the

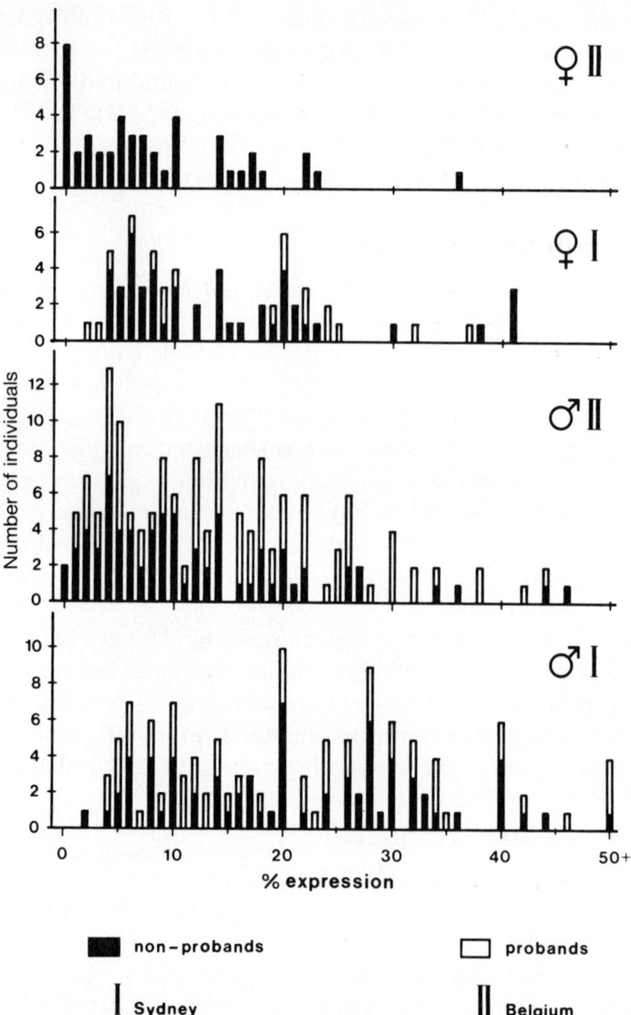

Fig. 5.3. Distribution of males and females in a Belgian and an Australian population with Martin–Bell syndrome according to their degree of expression of the fragile X (from Tommerup *et al.* 1988).

reported increase in the twinning rate in families with MB (Fryns 1986; Sherman *et al.* 1988).

Expression in normal male transmitters

Segregation analyses have suggested that 20 per cent of male carriers of the putative mutation are phenotypically normal (Sherman *et al.* 1985).

The majority of these male transmitters have not been available for chromosome analysis, since they have been identified retrospectively by the occurrence of mental retardation in their grandchildren. In those where a chromosome analysis has been made, the fragile X was either not expressed at all or only in a few per cent of the cells (Rhoads *et al.* 1982; Camerino *et al.* 1983; Froster-Iskenius *et al.* 1984; Lubs *et al.* 1984; Howard-Peebles and Friedman 1985; Steinbach 1986). However, some non- or low-expressing hemizygous males identified through their grandchildren may be explained by an age-related reduction in expression in less-affected males with an initial low expression of the fragile X (Turner and Partington 1988; see also Loesch *et al.* 1987).

The conclusion is that, apart from exceptional cases, high and reproducible expression of the fragile X ($\geqslant 4$ per cent) in males is associated with MB (Silverman *et al.* 1983). Also, it may not be possible to define a lower limit of expression associated with MB. To obtain as non-biased data as possible, all males in fragile X families should be cytogenetically examined irrespective of their phenotype, and at as young an age as possible.

Expression in affected females

One-third of heterozygous carriers are affected to some degree (Turner *et al.* 1980), which is an unusually large proportion for an X-linked disease. As a rule, the fragile X is more readily demonstrated in affected female carriers than in carriers with normal intelligence (Howard-Peebles 1980; Jacobs *et al.* 1980; Fishburn *et al.* 1983; Nielsen *et al.* 1983*b*; Knoll *et al.* 1984) with a median expression in the range 10–15 per cent (Fig. 5.3).

Expression in normal female carriers

Although one-tenth of normal female carriers also show high expression (Turner and Jacobs 1983), the fragile X can be demonstrated in only half of all obligate carriers. An inverse relationship between age and fragile X expression has been reported (Sutherland 1979*c*; Jacobs *et al.* 1980; Nielsen *et al.* 1983*b*). This absent expression in obligate carriers was not reversed by FdU (Brookwell *et al.* 1982; Nielsen *et al.* 1983*b*). Obligate carrier daughters of transmitting males have so far been considered to be unaffected, with no or very low expression of the fragile X (Lubs *et al.* 1984). At closer inspection, some of them may show features of the fragile X phenotype, including mental impairment, but still with absent or low expression of the fragile X (Loesch *et al.* 1987).

The role of X-inactivation

The question why some carrier females are affected while others are normal still remains unanswered. One possible explanation could be a difference in the X-inactivation pattern. An increased frequency of active, early replicating fragile X chromosomes in affected females, and an increased frequency of inactive, late replicating fragile X chromosomes in normal females have been observed in several studies (Howell and McDermott 1982; Uchida and Joyce 1982; Uchida *et al.* 1983; Knoll *et al.* 1984). The same pattern was found in a pair of MZ female twins with markedly discordant phenotypes (Tuckerman *et al.* 1985). However, in some studies, an excess of active fragile X chromosomes have been observed in both affected and normal females (Nielsen *et al.* 1983*b*; Fryns *et al.* 1984*a*; Fryns and Van den Berghe 1988*b*). An excess of fragile X expression on the active X chromosome was also observed following a late pulse with ^{3}H-dT (Lubs 1969). One reason for these observations could be that the late BrdU- or ^{3}H-dT-pulse used preferentially reduces the expression on the late-replicating inactive X chromosome. Support for this is that a late pulse of BrdU suppresses the expression of the fragile X in heterozygous, but not in hemizygous, carriers (Wilhelm *et al.* 1988).

To overcome possible effects of BrdU on the inactivation pattern, Van Dyke *et al.* (1986) used the Xq13-q21 bend as a marker for the inactive X (Flejter *et al.* 1984) and found a random fragile X inactivation pattern in both affected and normal carriers. However, the observation of the bend on both the active and inactive X chromsome questions the reliability of this method (T. Webb, pers. comm.).

Overall, a negative correlation between IQ scores and fragile X frequency on the active X chromosome have been found (Wilhelm *et al.* 1988), providing additional evidence that inactivation of the fragile X locus contributes to the phenotype in female carriers. Still, it is not possible in the single individual to predict mental development on the basis of the X-inactivation pattern (Nielsen *et al.* 1983*b*; Wilhelm *et al.* 1988).

Association with other chromosomal disorders

In view of the frequency of MB, it would not be surprising that this condition should be observed in combination with other common chromosomal disorders. However, some data suggest a non-random association between MB and aneuploidy involving the X chromosome. Klinefelter syndrome (47,XXY) in combination with the fragile X syndrome have been reported several times (Wilmot *et al.* 1980; Froster-Iskenius *et al.* 1982; Fryns *et al.* 1983, 1984*b*; Deb *et al.* 1987; Pueschel *et al.* 1987). Among 447 male fragile X patients, Fryns and Van den Berghe (1988*a*) observed three with concurrent Klinefelter syndrome, compared to the expected 1.18 per thousand. The incidence of the fragile X among 47,XXY individuals was also found to be several times higher than expected (Filippi *et al.* 1988). Cases with concurrent 45,X or 47,XXX and the fragile X have also been reported (e.g. von Koskull *et al.* 1985; Seemanova *et al.* 1985), but more systematic data are lacking. A ten times higher incidence of sex-chromosome aneuploidy was observed in PHA-stimulated PBL from female fragile X carriers (Nielsen 1986).

Concurrent observation of trisomy 21 and the fragile X has been reported (Jacobs *et al.* 1980; Arinami *et al.* 1987), and initial data may suggest an increased risk of trisomy 21 offspring to fragile X carriers (Watson *et al.* 1986). Larger series of well-characterized families should be compiled to prove or disprove this important suggestion.

Only sporadic cases with concurrent presence of a constitutional chromosome rearrangement and the fragile X have been reported (J. T. Hecht *et al.* 1983). The rearrangements have not involved the Xq27-region and this region is rarely involved in constitutional rearrangements observed at amniocentesis or in spontaneous abortions, still births, and new-borns (Hecht and Hecht 1984*a*, *b*).

Hypotheses and cytogenetics

Mothers and daughters of transmitting males have offspring who express the fragile X differently, with an apparently increased penetrance in succeeding generations (Sherman *et al.* 1984, 1985). This does not fit a regular X-linked recessive mode of inheritance, so a number of complex hypotheses have been formulated. In the following section some of these theories are discussed with emphasis on the cytogenetic data.

DNA repair; DNA recombination

Expression of the fragile X on both chromatids occurs following induction during a single replication cycle (Cantú and Jacobs 1984; Tommerup 1986). It has been suggested that the fragile X may be DNA which has not finished chromosomal condensation due to extensive DNA repair in the G_2 phase of the cell cycle (Nussbaum and Ledbetter 1986). Initially, uracil misincorporation/removal (Goulian *et al.* 1980; Sedwick *et al.* 1981) provided an attractive candidate for a repair mechanism due to the involvement of thymidylate deficiency in fragile X induction (Sutherland 1979*a*; Krumdieck and Howard-Peebles 1983). The involvement of uracil misincorporation was also suggested since deoxyuridine increased expression of folate-sensitive fragile sites (Reidy

1987). However, this type of repair would probably not be involved in induction by deoxycytidine deficiency (Sutherland *et al.* 1985), and uracil misincorporation into total DNA is within normal levels in fragile X cells (Wang *et al.* 1985).

Still, other types of DNA repair might be involved in expression. Caffeine, an inhibitor of postreplication DNA repair, caused a dramatic increase in fragile X expression in hybrid cells (Ledbetter *et al.* 1986*a, b, c*), whereas the effect in lymphocytes is less certain (Yunis and Soreng 1984; Abruzzo *et al.* 1986; Ledbetter *et al.* 1986*b*). Aphidicolin, a specific inhibitor of DNA polymerase α, and AraC, a competitive inhibitor of DNA polymerases, inhibited the induction of the fragile X by FdU and excess dT (Tommerup 1987*b*). Since the induction of the fragile X by FdU and excess thymidine occurs via inhibition of DNA replication, it is hard to explain why further inhibition by DNA polymerase inhibitors should decrease this expression, unless some type of DNA repair involving the α polymerase (Hanoka *et al.* 1979; van Zeeland *et al.* 1982) is involved in the expression of the fragile X.

An increased sensitivity towards the clastogenic effect of FdU was observed in lymphoblastoid cell lines from fragile X carriers (Duncan 1986). Although a normal level of sister chromatid exchanges (SCEs) per cell was found in carriers of the fragile X (Branda *et al.* 1984; Gregory *et al.* 1986; Wenger *et al.* 1987), an excess of SCEs occur in the Xq27 region in fragile X carriers (Glover and Stein 1987; Tommerup 1986, 1987*c*; Wenger *et al.* 1987) (Fig. 5.4). This is evidence of a localized increased mitotic recombination which could either be due to a high degree of DNA damage, e.g. in repetitive sequences, caused by the inducing conditions (nucleotide-pool imbalance), or a highly recombinogenic unique sequence may exist in the region. In any case, it is further evidence of the association between abnormal replication and fragile X expression.

Another cytogenetic observation which might be explained by somatic crossing-over within or near the fragile site (Gardner 1984) is the apparent homozygosity for the fragile X observed in a few cells from a phenotypically normal female carrier (Nielsen *et al.* 1982).

Premutation model

Pembrey *et al.* (1985) suggested the presence of a premutation in the normal male transmitters. This premutation then could be converted into the full mutation in the germ cells in their obligate carrier daughters by a meiotic cross-over event. The premutation might involve a submicroscopic chromosome rearrangement without ill effect *per se*, but which would generate genetic imbalance when involved in a recombination event with another X chromosome.

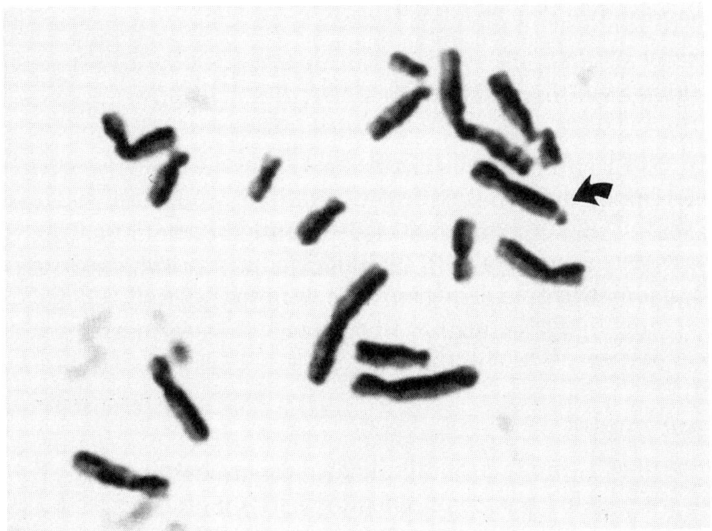

Fig. 5.4. Sister chromatid exchange (SCE) at the fragile site Xq27 (arrow).

Amplification model

Based on the mode of induction of the fragile X, it was proposed that the molecular basis of the fragile site might be specific polypurine/polypyrimidine sequences which were present in an unusual amount in fragile X individuals (Sutherland *et al.* 1985; Sutherland and Baker 1986). Along with this, Nussbaum *et al.* (1986*b*) proposed that the nature of the mutation might be amplification of specific repetitive sequences by unequal crossing over during female meiosis, i.e. in essence a modification of the premutation model.

When isolated in hybrid cells, the gradually increasing expression of fragility in the q27 region on X chromosomes derived from normal, transmitting, and affected males led to the suggestion that a common fragile site, normally present in this region, mutates step-wise to the full-blown mutation observed as the fragile X associated with MB (Ledbetter *et al.* 1986*c*; Nussbaum and Ledbetter 1986). The similar presence of fragility in a chimpanzee X chromosome suggested the involvement of an evolutionary conserved sequence.

Inactivation model

Laird (1987, 1988) proposed a mechanism where the fragile X mutation prevents the normally occurring reactivation of the inactive X chromosome during female oogenesis. A region around fragile X (q27) would remain inactive, and males receiving such an X chromosome would be functionally nullosomic for this part of the genome. In females, the proportion and distribution of the partially inactivated X chromosome which escaped X-inactivation during embryogenesis would determine the phenotype.

This type of chromosomal imprinting would probably involve differential DNA methylation. In initial studies, inhibition of fragile X expression by the DNA methylation inhibitor 5-azacytidine (azaC) was reported (Mixon and Dev 1983; Daniel *et al.* 1984*a*; Dev and Mixon 1984) but only when much higher concentrations of azaC than necessary for inhibition of DNA methylation were used (Abruzzo *et al.* 1985; Glover *et al.* 1986; Ledbetter *et al.* 1986*a*).

Deletion model

Warren (1988) proposed that the known fragility observed *in vitro* also occurs *in vivo.* Mental impairment would thus be related to the number of cells in the brain in which the Xq27–qter region was deleted. We have only indirect evidence from other types of tissue regarding the occurrence of fragility *in vivo.* Expression of the fragile X has not been observed in direct chromosome preparations from chorionic villus samples from affected fetuses; normal activity of G6PD was found in males with the fragile X (Carrol and Howard-Peebles 1981); one consequence of *in-vitro* fragility in the preceding cell cycle is the occurrence of triradial figures, which in lymphocytes have been observed only in cells which have replicated at least twice *in vitro* (Tommerup 1987*a*). Thus, we have, so far, no evidence for the occurrence of fragility *in vivo*, although this does not exclude that specific conditions may occur in the brain during fetal life.

Transposable elements/virus

The involvement of a transposable genetic element has been proposed (Nielsen *et al.* 1982; Friedman and Howard-Peebles 1986; Hoegerman and Rary 1986).

Two aspects may be mentioned in this connection:

1. The suspected non-random association between the fragile X and chromosomal non-disjunction; chromosomal non-disjunction is one feature of the hybrid dysgenesis associated with the P element in *Drosophila* (Kidwell *et al.* 1977).

2. The apparent frequent observation of other rare fragile sites in fragile X individuals (Sutherland and Hecht 1985) could be explained by transposition.

One of the first proposals was that the fragile X could represent a viral modification site (Giraud *et al.* 1976), due to its morphological resemblance to the known adenovirus modification sites at 17q21 and 1q42 (McDougall 1971).

Modifier loci

Steinbach (1986) and Israel (1987) independently suggested that an autosomal modifier locus might be involved.

In fragile X/hamster hybrid cell-lines, expression was not modulated by the hamster genome or by the absence of all other human chromosomes (Nussbaum *et al.* 1983; Warren and Davidson 1984). According to the modifier hypotheses, the decisive factor(s) determining whether males will be normal transmitters or affected, would be the alleles at the modifier locus (or loci). The modified locus at Xq27 would not be changed in subsequent generations. In that case, one would expect the same degree of expression of the fragile X, irrespective of the origin of an X chromosome isolated in cell hybrids. However, the opposite was observed, a gradual increased expression was found on X chromosome isolated from normal, transmitting, and affected males (Ledbetter *et al.* 1986*c*), suggesting that the decisive change is on the X chromosome. Furthermore, the fragility persisted even in hybrid subclones retaining very little of the X chromosome around the fragile site. (Nussbaum *et al.* 1986*a*; Warren *et al.* 1987).

X-linked dominance with incomplete penetrance

This would be the most simple model for the inheritance of MB. When attention was paid to less obvious dysmorphic features, a continuous rather than a bimodal (affected/non-affected) distribution of the fragile X phenotype among transmitting males and their carrier daughters was found in three families (Loesch *et al.* 1987). Still, the grandsons were more affected than their grandfathers, and it was suggested that at least some of this could be due to assortative mating with respect to intelligence. Although this may explain some of the apparent complexity with regard to the phenotype, this does not explain the association between the phenotype and the cytogenetic marker.

Cytogenetics in the future

New insight into the organization of this important part of the human genome will be provided by combining cytogenetic methods with molecular techniques as exemplified by *in situ* hybridization (Mattei *et al.* 1985; Patterson *et al.* 1987).

Some of the proposed models may be tested by cytogenetic techniques. If the fragile X syndrome involves structural chromosomal rearrangements, this may be disclosed by detailed analysis of the pairing behaviour in the X bivalent in fragile X positive female fetuses. One consequence of the inactivation model would be that a (variable) region around the fragile site should be inactive and late replicating (Laird *et al.* 1987), and this might be tested by high-resolution replication studies and *in situ* nick translation (Kerem *et al.* 1983). Mitotic recombination following *in vitro* induction (site-specific SCEs) might be related to the meiotic recombinational variability which has been observed between families with the fragile X syndrome (Brown *et al.* 1985, 1987).

It is hoped that molecular cloning of the fragile X will provide some of the many answers about this intriguing genetic phenomenon, and may provide the basis for more specific diagnostic methods. So far, the cytogenetic demonstration of the fragile X remains the method of choice for the diagnosis of this most common form of heritable mental handicap. Indeed, if the phenotype turns out to be determined by chromosomal imprinting, molecular methods for reliable diagnosis may be far off in the future.

Prenatal diagnosis

Pregnancies at risk

Prenatal diagnosis of the fragile X has primarily been offered to women with a family history of the syndrome. In some cases there has been a family history of MR, but without documented fragile X—in 38 cases of the latter type, Shapiro *et al.* (1988) did not find a single fragile X fetus. Whenever possible, affected individual(s) from such families should be examined for the fragile X prior to prenatal diagnosis. In families with a known fragile X it is often impossible to decide whether the pregnant woman is actually a carrier or not. Although the pregnancy *per se* does not seem to affect the expression of the fragile X (Tommerup *et al.* 1986*b*), carrier diagnosis by demonstration of the fragile X is so uncertain in unaffected females that prenatal diagnosis should be offered anyway. Some help may be offered by RFLP-diagnosis (Mulley and Sutherland 1987), but so far we would be reluctant to decide against a prenatal diagnosis due to RFLP data alone.

Occasionally, a fragile X-like lesion may be observed during routine prenatal diagnosis in pregnancies without any known risk of MB. In most of these cases, this appears to be a non-specific, single observation which cannot be reproduced (Shapiro *et al.* 1988). However, in two cases the presence of the fragile X was later confirmed (Tommerup *et al.* 1987*c*;

Jenkins *et al.* 1988), suggesting that such incidental observations should be pursued.

Males

Until the feasibility to demonstrate the fragile X in fetal cells was demonstrated (Jenkins *et al.* 1981; T. Webb *et al.* 1981; Shapiro *et al.* 1982), the only option for prenatal diagnosis in these families was selective abortion of all male fetuses. Still, MB *per se* cannot be diagnosed *in utero*, but demonstration of the associated fragile X is used as a marker for the disease in male fetuses. The implications of this are that, apart from the technical problems associated with the induction of the fragile X in fetal cells, we also have to rely on our present knowledge about the relation between expression and clinical status in children and adults when predicting the possible clinical status of a fetus. Thus, if the fragile X is demonstrated in a male fetus, we assume that it is a fetus with MB. If the expression in the fetal cells is very low, either due to genetic/ cellular characteristics or due to a technical artefact, this may lead to confusion with the occasionally occurring fragile X-like lesions in normal cells. Conversely, such non-specific lesions may lead to a false positive diagnosis.

Females

One-third of the female carriers are affected to some degree. Those affected generally show a higher frequency of the fragile X in PBL, but some normal females also have high expression. In normal female carriers, the fragile X cannot be demonstrated in half of the cases. In those where it is seen, the expression decreases with age, but we do not know the initial degree of expression in most of these cases. This, together with the possible effect of X-inactivation, at present makes it impossible, in a specific female fetus, to relate degree of expression with clinical status. Thus, prenatal prediction of the phenotype in fragile X positive females is not possible at the moment.

Prenatal diagnosis by RFLP-analysis

Prenatal diagnosis of MB by RFLP-analysis is possible in some cases (Oberlé *et al.* 1985), but the lack of closely linked DNA probes with a high information content indicates that cytogenetic screening for the fragile X is still the most reliable method. However, in approximately half of the cases RFLP-analysis can complement cytogenetic analysis (Tommerup *et al.* 1987*b*; Jenkins *et al.* 1988), and the isolation of new probes will undoubtedly increase the value of RFLP-analysis.

Present experiences

Prenatal diagnosis of the fragile X has been reported in at least 330 pregnancies at risk, including 242 by amniocentesis (Moric-Petrovic and Laca 1983; Tejada *et al.* 1983; Hogge *et al.* 1984; Venter *et al.* 1984; Wilson and Marchese 1984; von Koskull *et al.* 1985; Oberlé *et al.* 1985; Rocchi *et al.* 1985; Lindenberg *et al.* 1986; Schmidt and Passarge 1986; Tommerup *et al.* 1986*a*; Jenkins *et al.* 1988; Pervis-Smith *et al.* 1988; Shapiro *et al.* 1988). In at least 29 cases, fetal blood sampling has been used (Webb *et al.* 1987; McKinley *et al.* 1988; Shapiro *et al.* 1988), and in at least 63 pregnancies chorionic villi were used (von Koskull *et al.* 1985; Pergament *et al.* 1985; Sachs *et al.* 1985; Tommerup *et al.* 1985, 1987*b*; Jenkins *et al.* 1988; Purvis-Smith *et al.* 1988; Shapiro *et al.* 1988).

At least 45 fragile X positive males and 32 fragile X positive females have been detected. The vast majority of the pregnancies with positive male fetuses have been terminated (42/45), whereas the vast majority of the positive females have continued to term (31/32).

The technical problems associated with the induction of the fragile X, especially in amniocytes and cultured chorionic villus cells, are still of major concern. False negative and positive diagnosis of female fetuses (Moric-Petrovic and Laca 1983; Tommerup *et al.* 1986a; Jenkins *et al.* 1988; Purvis-Smith *et al.* 1988) may in part be associated with the generally low expression of the fragile X observed in PBL from many normal female carriers, and may thus turn out to be without major clinical consequences. However, at least two false negative analyses of male fetuses (Shapiro *et al.* 1988) have been reported with amniotic fluid cells. One prime example of the difficulty is illustrated by the discordant expression of the fragile X in amniocytes from male monozygous twins (0.4 per cent and 17.5 per cent positive cells), who had concordant (32 per cent and 34 per cent) expression in their lymphocytes (Rocchi *et al.* 1985). Also, there are several reports of discordant results on the same specimen which has been split between collaborating laboratories. The problem may be related to the heterogeneous origin of amniotic fluid cells.

False negative diagnoses of male fetuses have been described with chorionic villus cells in two cases in the same study (Shapiro *et al.* 1988). However, the same group also experienced culture failure in three out of 13 attempts, suggesting suboptimal culturing conditions. Other groups have found more reliable expression in cultured chorionic villus cells than in amniotic fluid cells (Tommerup *et al.* 1987*b*; Purvis-Smith *et al.* 1988). So far, expression of the fragile X has not been possible in direct or short-term CVS-cultures, and Chang medium inhibits fragile X expression even in the presence of FdU or excess thymidine (Jenkins *et al.* 1986*b*, 1988).

Although the world-wide experience with fetal blood is still limited, this method seems to be the least problematic from a cytogenetic point of view (no false negative/positive cases reported). However, the sampling technique is not so widely accessible.

Guidelines for prenatal diagnosis of the fragile X

Due to the inherent advantages of first trimester prenatal diagnosis, CVS as a widely accessible technique is recommended as the first alternative in pregnancies at risk for MB. Based on experience from a number of centres, the following guidelines for prenatal diagnosis are suggested:

1. The mother and key family members should ideally be tested before pregnancy to determine whether RFPL-analysis will be of help for prenatal diagnosis. Doing this before pregnancy may save time, and the size of the biopsy may depend on whether DNA should be extracted or not. However, in many cases RFLP-analysis has not been done before the pregnancy. Then the advantage with CVS is that DNA can be extracted directly from part of the biopsy without wasting time on cell culture.

2. Depending on the amount of tissue available, and experience of the lab, more than one lab should initiate and examine parallel cultures.

3. If fetal sexing indicates a female fetus, some centres do not proceed with the analysis. However, we examine all fetuses at risk to gain experience and to accumulate basic data for later evaluation of possible association between expression during fetal life and subsequent development; furthermore, the prenatal cases are an unbiased population which can be used for segregation analysis, and some families may want an exclusion diagnosis even for females.

4. Several separate cultures should be analysed. The excess thymidine method may well be the method of choice (Sutherland *et al.* 1987; Tommerup *et al.* 1987*b*; Tommerup 1988), but until more experience has been gained, the use of either FdU or MTX is also recommended.

5. If positive, at least two cultures should be positive before establishing the diagnosis.

6. If negative, at least 100–200 cells should be examined from separate cultures.

7. If negative in a male fetus, or in case of very low expression, second trimester diagnosis may be offered, preferably with fetal blood. This decision may depend on availability of low-risk fetal blood sampling, *a*

priori risk for the fetus, degree of expression in affected relatives, and outcome of RFLP-analysis.

8. It is expected that 20 per cent of all male carriers will be normal or only slightly affected male transmitters (Sherman *et al.* 1985; Loesch *et al.* 1987). Since they have very low or absent expression of the fragile X in adult life, it is possible that they will also be cytogenetically negative in fetal life. If so, discrepancy between RFLP data (possibly carrier) and cytogenetic data (negative) are expected to occur in 10 per cent of all male fetuses of obligate carrier mothers.

Possibly two such cases have been described (Tommerup *et al.* 1987*b*; Shapiro *et al.* 1988). Other explanations for such a discrepancy would be a double cross-over between the flanking markers or a cytogenetically false negative case. In such cases, we would offer fetal blood sampling and, if negative, we would deem that the fetus will be a (normal) male transmitter without significant phenotypic problems.

9. Follow-up studies on fetal cells in case of termination, and in cord blood/peripheral blood after birth, should be done in all cases studied.

In conclusion, prenatal diagnosis of MB by the demonstration of the fragile X is possible in males but not in females. Although not 100 per cent reliable, the diagnosis can be made with a fairly high degree of success, especially if techniques are combined. Due to the many technical and counselling problems, this is not a routine test, and as such should be offered by centres with special experience.

References

Abruzzo, M. A., Mayer, M., and Jacobs, P. A. (1985). The effect of methionine and 5-azacytidine on fragile X expression. *American Journal of Human Genetics*, **37**, 193–8.

Abruzzo, M. A., Pettay, D., Mayer, M., and Jacobs, P. A. (1986). The effect of caffeine on fragile X expression. *Human Genetics*, **73**, 20–2.

Arce, M. A. De (1983). Tables for the cytogenetic study of fragile X chromosomes for diagnostic purposes. *Clinical Genetics*, **24**, 320–3.

Arce, M. A. De, Hecht, F., Sutherland, G. R., and Webb, G. C. (1986). Guidelines for the diagnosis of fragile X. *Clinical Genetics*, **29**, 95.

Arinami, T., Kondo, I., and Nakajima, S. (1986). Frequency of the fragile X syndrome in Japanese mentally retarded males. *Human Genetics*, **73**, 309–12.

Arinami, T., Kondo, I., Hamaguchi, H., Tamura, K., and Hirano, T. (1987). A fragile X female with Down syndrome. *Human Genetics*, **77**, 92–4.

Barbi, G. and Steinbach, P. (1982). Increase in the incidence of the fragile site Xq27 in prometaphases. *Human Genetics*, **61**, 82.

Branda, R. F., Arthur, D. C., Woods, W. G., Danzl, T. J., and King, R. A. (1984).

Folate metabolism and chromosomal stability in the fragile X syndrome. *American Journal of Medicine*, **77**, 602–11.

Brookwell, R. and Turner, G. (1983). High resolution banding and the locus of the Xq fragile site. *Human Genetics*, **63**, 77.

Brookwell, R., Daniel, A., Turner, G., and Fishburn, J. (1982). The fragile X(q27) form of X-linked mental retardation. FUdR as an inducing agent for fra(X)(q27) expression in lymphocytes, fibroblasts and amniocytes. *American Journal of Medical Genetics*, **13**, 139–48.

Brown, W. T., *et al.* (1984). Folic acid therapy in the fragile X syndrome. *American Journal of Medical Genetics*, **17**, 289–97.

Brown, W. T., Gross, A. C., Chan, C. B., and Jenkins, E. C. (1985). Genetic linkage heterogeneity in the fragile X syndrome. *Human Genetics*, **71**, 11–18.

Brown, W. T. *et al.* (1986). High dose folic acid treatment of fragile(X) males. *American Journal of Medical Genetics*, **23**, 263–72.

Brown, W. T., *et. al.* (1987). Further evidence for genetic heterogeneity in the fragile X syndrome. *Human Genetics*, **75**, 311–21.

Calva-Mercado, M., Maunoury, C., Rethoré, M., and Lejeune, J. (1983). Fragilité de l'X et inhibition de la dihydrofolate reductase. Comparaison des effets de deux antibiotiques: triméthoprime et pyrimethamine. *Annales de Génétique*, **26**, 147–9.

Camerino, G., Mattei, M. G., Mattei, J. F., Jaye, M., and Mandel, J. L. (1983). Close linkage of fragile X-mental retardation syndrome to haemophilia B and transmission through a normal male. *Nature*, **306**, 701–4.

Cantú, E. S. and Jacobs, P. A. (1984). Fragile (X) expression: relationship to the cell cycle. *Human Genetics*, **67**, 99–102.

Cantú, E. S., Nussbaum, R. L., Airhart, S. D., and Ledbetter, D. H. (1985). Fragile (X) expression induced by FUdR is transient and inversely related to levels of thymidylate synthase activity. *American Journal of Human Genetics*, **37**, 947–55.

Carroll, A. J. and Howard-Peebles, P. N. (1981). Normal activity and electrophoretic mobility of erythrocyte glucose-6-phosphate dehydrogenase in males with X-linked mental retardation and the fragile Xq. *American Journal of Human Genetics*, **33**, 826–8.

Chudley, A. E., Knoll, J., Gerrard, J. W., Shepel, L., McGahey, E., and Anderson, J. (1983). Fragile (X) X-linked mental retardation I: relationship between age and intelligence and the frequency of expression of fragile-(X) (q28). *American Journal of Medical Genetics*, **14**, 699–712.

Daker, M. G., Chidiac, P., Fear, C. N., and Berry, A. C. (1981). Fragile X in a normal male: a cautionary tale. *Lancet*, **i**, 780.

Daniel, A., Ekblom, L., and Phillips, S. (1984*a*). Fragile X expression suppressed in either FUdR or methotrexate treated fibroblasts by pretreatment with 5-azacytidine. *American Journal of Medical Genetics*, **17**, 225–57.

Daniel, A., Ekblom, L., and Phillips, S. (1984*b*). Constitutive fragile sites 1p31, 3p14, 6q26 and 16q23 and their use as controls for false-negative results with the fragile (X). *American Journal of Medical Genetics*, **18**, 483–91.

Deb, S., Cowie, V. A., and Timberlake, C. (1987). A case of mosaicism with fragile-X and XXY Components. *British Journal of Psychiatry*, **150**, 700–2.

Dev, V. G. and Mixon, C. (1984). 5-azacytidine decreases the frequency of fragile X expression in peripheral lymphocyte culture. *American Journal of Medical Genetics*, **17**, 253–4.

Duncan, A. M. V. (1986). Enhanced sensitivity of lymphoblastoid cells from individuals carrying the mutation for the fragile X syndrome to the clastogenic effects of FUdR. *Mutation Research*, **173**, 201–5.

Dyke, D. L. van. *et al.* (1986). A practical metaphase marker of the inactive X chromosome. *American Journal of Human Genetics*, **39**, 88–95.

Eberle, G., Zankl, M., and Zankl, H. (1982*b*). The expression of fragile X chromosomes in members of the same family at different times of examination. *Human Genetics*, **61**, 254–5.

Erbe, R. W. (1984). Folic acid therapy in the fragile X syndrome. *American Journal of Medical Genetics*, **17**, 299–301.

Escalanté, J. A., Grunspun, H., and Frota-Pessoa, O. (1971). Severe sex-linked mental retardation. *Journal de Génétique Humaine*, **19**, 137.

Ferguson-Smith, M. A. (1977). Human chromosome polymorphism. *Records of the Adelaide Children's Hospital*, **1**, 278–86.

Filippi, G., Pecile, V., Rinaldi, A., and Siniscalco, M. (1988). Fragile-X mutation and Klinefelter's syndrome: A reappraisal. *American Journal of Medical Genetics*, **30**, 99–107.

Fishburn, J., Turner, G., Daniel, A., and Brookwell, R. (1983). The diagnosis and frequency of X-linked conditions in a cohort of moderately retarded males with affected brothers. *American Journal of Medical Genetics*, **14**, 713–24.

Fitchett, M. and Seabright, M. (1984). Deleted X chromosomes in patients with the fragile X syndrome. *Journal of Medical Genetics*, **21**, 373.

Flejter, W. L., Dyke, D. L. van, and Weiss, L. (1984). Bends in human mitotic metaphase chromosomes, including a band marking the X-inactivation center. *ian Journal of Human Genetics*, **36**, 218–26.

Fonatsch, C. (1981). Chromosome banding in X-linked mental retardation. *Lancet*, **i**, 494.

Fonatsch, C. and Schwinger, E. (1983). Frequency of fragile X chromosomes, fra(X), in lymphocytes in relation to blood storage time and culture techniques. *Human Genetics*, **64**, 39–41.

Ford, C. E. and Madan, K. (1973). Branched chromosomes. An alternative to the hypothesis of selective endoreduplication. In *Chromosome identification, Nobel Symposium 23*, (ed. T. Caspersson and L. Zech), pp. 98–103. Academic Press, New York.

Friedman, J. M. and Howard-Peebles, P. N. (1986). Inheritance of fragile X syndrome: A hypothesis. *American Journal of Medical Genetics*, **23**, 701–14.

Froster-Iskenius, U., Schwinger, E., Weigert, M., and Fonatsch, C. (1982). Replication pattern in XXY cells with fra(X). *Human Genetics*, **60**, 278–80.

Froster-Iskenius, U., Schulze, A., and Schwinger, E. (1984). Transmission of the marker X syndrome trait by unaffected males: Conclusions from studies of large families. *Human Genetics*, **67**, 419–27.

Froster-Iskenius, U., Bodeker, K., Oepen, T., Matthes, R., Piper, U., and Schwinger, E. (1986). Folic acid treatment in males and females with fragile-(X)-syndrome. *American Journal of Medical Genetics*, **23**, 273–90.

Fryns, J. P. (1986). The female and the fragile X. A study of 144 obligate female carriers. *American Journal of Medical Genetics*, **23**, 157–69.

Fryns, J. P. and Berghe, H. van den (1988*a*). The concurrence of Klinefelter syndrome and fragile X syndrome. *American Journal of Medical Genetics*, **30**, 109–13.

Fryns, J. P. and Berghe, H. van den (1988*b*). Inactivation pattern of the fragile X in heterozygous carriers. *American Journal of Medical Genetics*, **30**, 401–6.

Fryns, J. P. *et al.* (1983). XY/XXY mosaicism and fragile X syndrome. *Annales de Génétique*, **26**, 251–3.

Fryns, J. P., Kleczkowska, A., Kubién, E., Petit, P., and Berghe, H. van den1(1984*a*). Inactivation pattern of the fragile X in heterozygous carriers. *Human Genetics*, **65**, 401–5.

Fryns, J. P., Kleczkowska, A., Wolfs, I., and Berghe, H. van den (1984*b*). Klinefelter syndrome and two fragile X chromosomes. *Clinical Genetics*, **26**, 445–7.

Gardiner, G. B., Wenger, S. L., and Steele, M. W. (1984). *In vitro* reversal of fragile-X expression by exogeneous thymidine. *Clinical Genetics*, **25**, 135–9.

Gardner, R. J. M. (1984). Fragile X "homozygosity" due to somatic crossing-over? *Human Genetics*, **66**, 100.

Gillberg, C. (1983). Identical triplets with infantile autism and the fragile-X syndrome. *British Journal of Psychiatry*, **143**, 256–60.

Giraud, F., Aymé, S., Mattei, J. F., Mattie, M. G. (1976). Constitutional chromosal breakage. *Human Genetics*, **34**, 125–36.

Glover, T. W. (1981). FUdR induction of the X chromosome fragile site: Evidence for the mechanism of folic acid and thymidine inhibition. *American Journal of Human Genetics*, **33**, 234–42.

Glover, T. W. and Howard-Peebles, P. N. (1983). The combined effects of FUdR addition and methionine depletion on the X-chromosome fragile site. *American Journal of Human Genetics*, **35**, 117–22.

Glover, T. W. and Stein, C. K. (1987). Induction of sister chromatid exchanges in common fragile sites. *American Journal of Human Genetics*, **41**, 882–90.

Glover, T. W., Coyle-Morris, J., Pearce-Birge, L., Berger, C., and Gemmill, R. M. (1986). DNA demethylation induced by 5-azacytidine does not affect fragile X expression. *American Journal of Human Genetics*, **38**, 309–18.

Goulian, M., Bleile, B., and Tseng, B. Y. (1980). Methotrexate-induced mis-incorporation of uracil into DNA. *Proceedings of the National Academy of Sciences USA*, **77**, 1956–60.

Gregory, P., Wang, N., and Howard-Peebles, P. N. (1986). Analysis of sister chromatid exhanges in fra(X) individuals. *American Journal of Medical Genetics*, **23**, 563–6.

Gustavson, K.-H., Dahlbom, K., Flood, A., Holmgren, G., Blomquist, H. K., and Sanner, G. (1985). Effect of folic acid treatment in the fragile X syndrome. *Clinical Genetics*, **27**, 463–7.

Hagen, C. B., van der, Ørstavik, K. H., Bakke, J., and Berg, K. (1983). Monozygous male triplets with mental retardation and a fragile X chromosome. *Clinical Genetics*, **23**, 232.

Hagerman, R. *et al.* (1983). Folic acid treatment of the fragile-X syndrome.

American Journal of Human Genetics, **35**, 92A.

Hagerman, R. J. *et al.* (1986). Oral folic acid versus placebo in the treatment of males with the fragile X syndrome. *American Journal of Medical Genetics*, **23**, 241–62.

Hanoka, F., Kata, H., Ikegami, S., Ohashi, M., and Yamoda, M. (1979). Aphidicolin does inhibit repair replication in Hela cells. *Biochemical Biophysical Research Communications*, **87**, 575–80.

Harrison, C. J., Jack, E. M., Allen, T. D., and Harris, R. (1983). The fragile X: A scanning electron microscope study. *Journal of Medical Genetics*, **20**, 280–5.

Harvey, J., Judge, C., and Wiener, S. (1977). Familial X-linked mental retardation with an X chromosome abnormality. *Journal of Medical Genetics*, **14**, 46–50.

Hecht, F., and Glover, T. W. (1983). Antibiotics trimethoprim and the fragile X chromosome. *New England Journal of Medicine*, **308**, 285–6.

Hecht, F. and Hecht, B. K. (1984*a*). Fragile sites and chromosome breakpoints in constitutional rearrangements I. Amniocentesis. *Clinical Genetics*, **26**, 169–73.

Hecht, F. and Hecht, B. K. (1984*b*). Fragile sites and chromosome breakpoints in constitutional rearrangements II. Spontaneous abortions, stillbirths and newborns. *Clinical Genetics*, **26**, 174–7.

Hecht, F., and Sutherland, G. R. (1984). Detection of the fragile X chromosome and other fragile sites. *Clinical Genetics*, **26**, 301–3.

Hecht, F., Jacky, P. B., and Sutherland, G. R. (1982). The fragile X chromosome: Current methods. *American Journal of Medical Genetics*, **11**, 489–95.

Hecht, F., Fryns, J. P., Vlietinick, R. F., and Berghe, H. van den (1986). Genetic control over fragile X chromosome expression. *Clinical Genetics*, **29**, 191–5.

Hecht, J. T., Scott, C. I., Butler, I. J., Moore, C. M. (1983). X-linked mental retardation with fragile site at band Xq2800. *Lancet*, **i**, 986.

Hoegerman, S. F. and Rary, J. M. (1986). Speculation on the role of transposable elements in human genetic disease with particular attention to achondroplasia and the fragile X syndrome. *American Journal of Medical Genetics*, **23**, 685–700.

Hogge, W. A., Schonberg, S. A., Glover, T. W., Hecht, F., and Golbus, M. S. (1984). Prenatal diagnosis of fragile (X) syndrome. *Obstetrics and Gynecology*, **63**, 195–215.

Hori, T., Ayusawa, D., Glover, T. W., and Seno, T. (1985). Expression of fragile site on the human X chromosome in somatic cell hybrids between human fragile X cells and thymidylate synthase-negative mouse mutant cells. *Japanese Journal of Cancer Research*, **76**, 977–83.

Howard-Peebles, P. N. (1980*a*). Fragile sites on human chromosomes. II. Demonstration of the fragile site Xq27 in carriers of X-linked mental retardation. *American Journal of Medical Genetics*, **7**, 497–501.

Howard-Peebles, P. N. (1981). Chromosome banding in X-linked mental retardation. *Lancet*, **i**, 494.

Howard-Peebles, P. N. (1986). Methionine metabolism and fragile X expression. *American Journal of Medical Genetics*, **23**, 511–14.

Howard-Peebles, P. N. and Friedman, J. M. (1985). Unaffected carrier males in families with fragile X syndrome. *American Journal of Human Genetics*, **37**,

956–64.

Howard-Peebles, P. N. and Pryor, J. C. (1981). Fragile sites on human chromosomes. I. The effect of methionine on the Xq fragile site. *Clinical Genetics*, **19**, 228–32.

Howell, R. T. and McDermott, A. (1982). Replication status of the fragile X chromosome, fra(X)(q27), in three heterozygous females. *Human Genetics*, **62**, 282–4.

Israel, M. H. (1987). Autosomal suppressor gene for fragile-X: an hypothesis. *American Journal of Medical Genetics*, **26**, 19–31.

Jacky, P. B. and Sutherland, G. R. (1983). Thymidylate synthetase inhibition and fragile site expression in lymphocytes. *American Journal of Human Genetics*, **35**, 1276–83.

Jacobs, P. A. *et al.* (1980). X-linked mental retardation: a study of 7 families. *American Journal of Medical Genetics*, **7**, 471–89.

Jalbert, H. *et al.* (1983). L'encephalopathie liée à la fragilite de l'X: Ni inactivation, ni deletion du fragment distal q28-qter arguments enzymatiques et morphometriques. *Journal de Génétique Humaine*, **31**, 133–9.

Jenkins, E. C. *et al.* (1981). Feasibility of fragile X chromosome prenatal diagnosis demonstrated. *Lancet*, **ii**, 1292.

Jenkins, E. C. *et al.* (1986*a*). Low frequency of apparently fragile X chromosomes in normal controls cultures: A possible explanation. *Experimental Cell Biology*, **54**, 40–8.

Jenkins, E. C. *et al.* (1986*b*). The prenatal detection of the fragile X chromosome: Review of recent experience. *American Journal of Medical Genetics*, **23**, 297–312.

Jenkins, E. C., Duncan, C. J., Krawczun, M. S., Berns, L. M., Sanz, M. M., and Brown, W. T. (1986*c*). Frequency of tri- or multiradial configurations in fragile X identification. *American Journal of Medical Genetics*, **23**, 531–6.

Jenkins, E. C., Kastin, B. R., Krawczun, M. S., Lele, K. P., Silverman, W. P., and Brown, W. T. (1986*d*). Fragile X chromosome frequency is consistent temporally and within replicate cultures. *American Journal of Medical Genetics*, **23**, 475–82.

Jenkins, E. C. *et al.* (1988). Recent experience in prenatal fra(X) detection. *American Journal of Medical Genetics*, **30**, 329–36.

Jennings, M., Hall, J. G., and Joehn, H. (1980). Significance of phenotypic and chromosomal abnormalities in X-linked mental retardation (Martin–Bell or Renpennin syndrome). *American Journal of Medical Genetics*, **7**, 417–32.

Kähkönen, M. *et al.* (1987). *Prevalance of the fragile X syndrome.* Abstract, Third International Workshop on the Fragile X and X-linked Mental Retardation. Troina, 13–16 September.

Kerem, B. S., Goitein, R., Richler, C., Marcus, M., and Cedar, H. (1983). *In situ* nick-translation distinguishes between active and inactive X chromosomes. *Nature*, **304**, 88–90.

Kidwell, M. G., Kidwell, J. F., and Sved, J. A. (1977). Hybrid dysgenesis in *Drosophila melanogaster.* A syndrome of aberrant traits including mutation, sterility and male recombination. *Genetics*, **86**, 813–33.

Knoll, J. H., Chudley, A. E., and Gerrard, J. W. (1984). Fragile (X) X-linked mental retardation. II Frequency and replication pattern of fragile (X)(q28) in heterozygotes. *American Journal of Human Genetics*, **36**, 640–5.

Koskull, H. von and Nordström, A.-M. (1987). *Cytogenetic fra(X) expression and linkage studies in eight Finnish fra(X) families.* Abstract, Third International Workshop on the Fragile X and X-linked Mental Retardation. Troina, 13–16 September.

Koskull, H. von Ämmälä, P., Nordström, A.-M., and Rapola, J. (1985). Improved technique for the expression of fragile-X in cultured amniotic fluid cells. *Human Genetics*, **69**, 218–23.

Krawczun, M. S., Jenkins, E. C., and Brown, W. T. (1985). Analysis of the fragile-X chromosome: localization and detection of the fragile site in high resolution preparations. *Human Genetics*, **69**, 209–11.

Krawczun, M. S., Lele, K. P., Jenkins, E. C., and Brown, W. T. (1986). Fragile X expression increased by low cell-culture density. *American Journal of Medical Genetics*, **23**, 467–74.

Krumdieck, C. L. and Howard-Peebles, P. N. (1983). On the nature of folic-acid-sensitive fragile sites in human chromosomes: a hypothesis. *American Journal of Medical Genetics*, **16**, 23–8.

Laird, C. D. (1987). Proposed mechanism of inheritance and expression of the human fragile X syndrome of mental retardation. *Genetics*, **117**, 587–99.

Laird, C. D. (1988). Fragile-X mutation proposed to block complete reactivation in females of an inactive X chromosome. *American Journal of Medical Genetics*, **30**, 693–6.

Laird, C., Jaffe, E., Karpen, G., Lamb, M., and Nelson, R. (1987). Fragile sites in human chromosomes as regions of late-replicating DNA. *Trends in Genetics*, **3**, 274–81.

Ledbetter, D. H. and Ledbetter, S. A. (1987). *High levels of fragile X expression in normal males induced by aphidicolin.* Abstract, Third International Workshop on the Fragile X and X-linked Mental Retardation. Troina, 13–16 September.

Ledbetter, D. H., Airhart, S. D., and Nussbaum, R. L. (1986*a*). Somatic cell hybrid studies of fragile(X) expression in a carrier female and transmitting male. *American Journal of Medical Genetics*, **23**, 429–44.

Ledbetter, D. H., Airhart, S. D., and Nussbaum, R. L. (1986*b*). Caffeine enhances fragile (X) expression in somatic cell hybrids. *American Journal of Medical Genetics*, **23**, 445–56.

Ledbetter, D. H., Ledbetter, S. A., and Nussbaum, R. L. (1986*c*). Implications of fragile X expression in normal males for the nature of the mutation. *Nature*, **324**, 161–3.

Lejeune, J., Manoury, C., Rethoré, M. O., Prieur, M., and Raoul, O. (1981). Site fragile Xq27 et métabolisme de monocarbones: Diminution significative de la fréquence de la lacune chromosomique par traitement *in vitro* et *in vivo. Comptes Rendus de l'Académie des Sciences (Sér D.) (Paris)*, **292**, 491–3.

Lejeune, J., Legrand, N., Lafourcade, J., Rethore, M. O., Raoul, O., Manuoury, C. (1982). Fragilité du chromosome X et effets de la triméthoprime. *Annales de Génétique*, **25**,149–51.

Leversha, M. A., Webb, G. C. and Pavey, S. M. (1981). Chromosome banding required for studies on X-linked mental retardation. *Lancet*, **i**, 49.

Lindenberg, S., Anderson, A. M., Thomsen, S. G., Hagen, C. B. van der (1986). Prænatal diagnostik af fragilt X-syndrom—Martin–Bell's syndrom. *Ugeskrift for Laeger*, **148**, 134–5.

Loesch, D. Z., Hay, D. A., Sutherland, G. R., Halliday, J., Judge, C., and Webb, G. C. (1987). Phenotypic variation in male-transmitted fragile X: genetic inferences. *American Journal of Medical Genetics*, **27**, 401–17.

Lubs, H. A. (1969). A marker X chromosome. *American Journal of Human Genetics*, **21**, 231–44.

Lubs, H. A., Lujan, J. E., Donahue, R., and Lubs, M. L. (1984). Diminished frequency of marker X and mental retardation after transmission through males. *American Journal of Human Genetics*, **36**, 102.

McDougall, J. K. (1971). Adenovirus-induced chromosome aberrations in human cells. *Journal of General Virology*, **12**, 43–51.

McKinley, M. J., Kearney, L. U., Nicolaides, K. H., Gosden, C. M., and Webb, T. P. (1988). Prenatal diagnosis of fragile X syndrome by placental (chorionic villi) biopsy culture. *American Journal of Medical Genetics*, **30**, 355–68.

Martin, J. O. and Bell, J. (1943). A pedigree of mental defect showing sex-linkage. *Archives of Neurology and Psychiatry*, **6**, 154–7.

Matoth, Y., Pinkas, A., Zamir, R., Mooallem, F., and Grossowicz, N. (1964). Studies on folic acid in infancy. *Pediatrics*, **33**, 507–11.

Mattei, M. G., Mattei, J.-F., Vidal, I., and Giraud, F. (1981). Expression in lymphocyte and fibroblast culture of the fragile X chromosome: a new technical approach. *Human Genetics*, **59**, 166–9.

Mattei, M. G. *et al.* (1985). Localization by *in situ* hybridization of the coagulation factor IX gene and of two polymorphic DNA probes with respect to the fragile X site. *Human Genetics*, **69**, 327–31.

Mixon, C. and Dev, V. G. (1983). Fragile X expression is decreased by 5-azacytidine and by S-adenosylhomocysteine. *American Journal of Human Genetics*, **35**, 1270–5.

Moric'-Petrovic', S. and Laca, Z. (1983). A father and daughter with fragile X chromosome. *Journal of Medical Genetics*, **20**, 476.

Mulley, J. C. and Sutherland, G. R. (1987). Fragile X transmission and the determination of carrier probabilities for genetic counselling. *American Journal of Medical Genetics*, **26**, 987–90.

Nielsen, K. B. (1986). Sex chromosome aneuploidy in fragile X carriers. *American Journal of Medical Genetics*, **23**, 537–44.

Nielsen, K. B. and Tommerup, N. (1984). Cytogenetic investigations in mentally retarded and normal males from 14 families with the fragile site at Xq28. Result of folic acid treatment on fra(X) expression. *Human Genetics*, **66**, 225–9.

Nielsen, K. B., Tommerup, N., Poulsen, H., and Mikkelsen, M. (1982). Apparent homozygosity for the fragile site at Xq28 in a normal female. *Human Genetics*, **61**, 60–2.

Nielsen, K. B., Tommerup, N., Frilis, B., Hjelt, K., and Hippe, E. (1983*a*). Folic acid metabolism in a patient with fragile X. *Clinical Genetics*, **24**, 153–5.

Nielsen, K. B., Tommerup, N., Poulsen, H., Jacobsen, P., Beck, B., and Mikkelsen,

M. (1983*b*). Carrier detection and X-inactivation studies in the fragile X syndrome. Cytogenetic studies in 63 obligate and potential carriers of the fragile X. *Human Genetics*, **64**, 240–5.

Noel, B., Quack, B., Mottet, J., Nantois, Y., and Dutrillaux, B. (1977). Selective endoreduplication or branched chromosome? *Experimental Cell Research*, **104**, 423–6.

Nussbaum, R. L. and Ledbetter, D. H. (1986). Fragile X syndrome: a unique mutation in man. *Annual Review of Genetics*, **20**, 109–45.

Nussbaum, R. L., Airhart, S. D., and Ledbetter, D. H. (1983). Expression of the fragile (X) chromosome in an interspecific somatic cell hybrid. *Human Genetics*, **64**, 148–50.

Nussbaum, R. L., Walmsley, R. M., Lesko, J. G., Airhart, S. D., and Ledbetter, D. H. (1985). Thymidylate synthase-deficient Chinese hamster cells: a selection system for human chromosome 18 and experimental system for the study of thymidylate synthase regulation and fragile X expression. *American Journal of Human Genetics*, **37**, 1192–205.

Nussbaum, R. L., Airhart, S. D., and Ledbetter, D. H. (1986*a*). A rodent-human hybrid containing Xq24-qter translocated to a hamster chromosome expresses the Xq27 folate-sensitive fragile site. *American Journal of Medical Genetics*, **23**, 457–66.

Nussbaum, R. L., Airhart, S. D., and Ledbetter, D. H. (1986*b*). Recombination and amplification of pyrimidine-rich sequences may be responsible for initiation and progression of the Xq27 fragile site: an hypothesis. *American Journal of Medical Genetics*, **23**, 715–22.

Oberlé, I., Mandel, J. L., Boué, J., Mattei, M. G., and Mattei, J. F. (1985). Polymorphic DNA markers in prenatal diagnosis of fragile X syndrome. *Lancet*, **i**, 871.

Patterson, M., Kenwrick, S., Thibodeau, S., Faulk, K., Mattei, J. F., and Davies, K. E. (1987). Mapping of DNA markers close to the fragile site on the human X chromosome at Xq27.3. *Nucleic Acids Research*, **15**, 2639–51.

Pembrey, M. E., Winter, R. M., and Davies, K. E. (1985). A premutation that generates a defect at crossing over explains the inheritance of fragile X mental retardation. *American Journal of Medical Genetics*, **21**, 709–17.

Pergament, E., Verlinsky, Y., Ginsberg, N. A., Cadkin, A., and Brandt, T. (1985). Assessment of the safety and accuracy of chorionic villi sampling in first trimester fetal diagnosis. In *First trimester fetal diagnosis*, (ed. M. Fraccaro, G. Simoni, and B. Brambati), pp. 314–20. Springer-Verlag, Berlin.

Popovich, B. W., Rosenblatt, D. S., Cooper, B. A., and Vekemans, M. (1983). Intracellular folate distribution in cultured fibroblasts from patients with the fragile X syndrome. *American Journal of Human Genetics*, **35**, 869–78.

Proops, R. and Webb, T. (1981). The 'fragile' X chromosome in the Martin–Bell–Renpenning syndrome and in males with other forms of familial mental retardation. *Journal of Medical Genetics*, **18**, 366–73.

Pueschel, S. M., O'Brien, M. M., and Padre-Mendoza, T. (1987). Klinefelter syndrome and associated fragile-X syndrome. *Journal of Mental Deficiency Research*, **31**, 73–9.

Purvis-Smith, S. G., Laing, S., Sutherland, G. R., and Baker, E. (1988). Prenatal diagnosis of the fragile X—the Australasian experience. *American Journal of Medical Genetics*, **30**, 337–45.

Reichard, P., Canellakis, Z. N., and Canellakis, E. S. (1961). Studies on a possible regulatory mechanism for the biosynthesis of deoxyribonucleic acid. *Journal of Biological Chemistry*, **236**, 2514–19.

Reidy, J. A. (1984). Folate, methionine, and the fragile X chromosome. *American Journal of Human Genetics*, **36**, 477–9.

Reidy, J. A. (1987). Deoxyuridine increases folate-sensitive fragile site expression in human lymphocytes. *American Journal of Medical Genetics*, **26**, 1–5.

Rhoads, F. A., Ogleby, A. C., Mayer, M., and Jacobs, P. A. (1982). Marker X syndrome in an oriental family with probable transmission by a normal male. *American Journal of Medical Genetics*, **12**, 205–17.

Richards, B. W., Sylvester, P. E., and Brooker, C. (1981). Fragile X-linked mental retardation: the Martin–Bell syndrome. *Journal of Mental Deficiency Research*, **25**, 253–6.

Rocchi, M., Pecile, V., Archidiacono, N., Monni, G., and Filippi, G. (1985). Prenatal diagnosis of the fragile-X in male monozygotic twins: discordant expression of the fragile site in amniocytes. *Prenatal Diagnosis*, **5**, 229–31.

Rosenblatt, D. S. *et al.* (1985). Folic acid blinded trial in identical twins with fragile X syndrome. *American Journal of Human Genetics*, **37**, 543–52.

Sachs, E. S., Hemel, J. O. van, Jahoda, M. G. J., and Galjaard, H. (1985). Results of 180 first trimester direct chromosome studies in chorionic villi. In *First trimester fetal diagnosis*, (ed. M. Fraccaro, G. Simoni, and B. Brambati), pp. 121–9. Springer-Verlag, Berlin.

Schmidt, A. and Passarge, E. (1986). Differential expression of fragile site Xq27 in cultured fibroblasts from hemizygotes and heterozygotes and its implications for prenatal diagnosis. *American Journal of Medical Genetics*, **23**, 515–26.

Sedwick, W. D., Kutler, M., and Brown, O. E. (1981). Antifolate-induced misincorporation of deoxyuridine monophosphate into DNA: Inhibition of high molecular weight DNA synthesis in human lymphoblastoid cells. *Proceedings of the National Academy of Sciences USA*, **78**, 917–21.

Seemanová, E., Schmidt, A., Subrt, I., Passarge, E., Macek, M., and Nedomová, V. (1985). The syndrome 47,XXX in a family with the fragile X chromosome syndrome. *Casopis Le'karu Ceských*, **124**, 988–91. [In Czech.]

Shapiro, L. R. *et al.* (1982). Prenatal diagnosis of fragile X chromosome. *Lancet*, **i**, 99–100.

Shapiro, L. R., Wilmot, P. L., Murphy, P. D., and Breg, W. G. (1988). Experience with multiple approaches to the prenatal diagnosis of the fragile X syndrome: Amniotic fluid, chorionic villi, fetal blood and molecular methods. *American Journal of Medical Genetics*, **30**, 347–54.

Sherman, S. L., Morton, N. E., Jacobs, P. A., Turner, G. (1984). The marker (X) syndrome: A cytogenetic and genetic analysis. *Annals of Human Genetics*, **48**, 21–37.

Sherman, S. L. *et al.* (1985). Further segregation analysis of the fragile X syndrome with special reference to transmitting males. *Human Genetics*, **69**, 289–99.

Sherman, S. L., Turner, G., Sheffield, R., Laing, S., and Robinson, H. (1988). Investigation of the twinning rate in families with the fragile X syndrome. *American Journal of Medical Genetics*, **30**, 625–31.

Silverman, W., Lubin, R., Jenkins, E. C., and Brown, T. (1983). The strength of association between fragile(X) chromosome presence and mental retardation. *Clinical Genetics*, **23**, 436–40.

Soudek, D. (1985). Decrease of fragile X frequence in stored blood samples; individual variability. *Clinical Genetics*, **28**, 399–400.

Soudek, D. (1986). Fragile X; experience of a laboratory. *Clinical Genetics*, **30**, 346–7.

Soudek, D. and Gorzny, N. (1980). No "fragile X" chromosome in normal men. *Clinical Genetics*, **19**, 140–1.

Soudek, D. and McGregor, T. (1981). Sources of error in fragile-X determination. *Lancet*, **i**, 556–7.

Soudek, D., Partington, M. W., and Lawsonn, J. S. (1984). The fragile X syndrome I: familial variation in the proportion of lymphocytes with the fragile site in males. *American Journal of Human Genetics*, **17**, 241–52.

Soysa, P., Senanayahe, M., Mikkelsen, M., and Poulsen, H. (1982). Martin–Bell syndrome fra(X)(q28) in a Sri Lankan family. *Journal of Mental Deficiency Research*, **26**, 251–7.

Steinbach, P., Barbi, G., and Boller, T. (1982). On the frequency of telomeric chromosomal changes induced by culture conditions suitable for fragile X expressions. *Human Genetics*, **61**, 160–2.

Steinbach, P., Barbi, G., Baur, S., and Wiedenmann, A. (1983). Expression of the fragile site Xq27 in fibroblasts. I. Detection of fra(X)(q27) in fibroblasts clones from males with X-linked mental retardation. *Human Genetics*, **63**, 404–5.

Steinbach, P. (1986). Mental impairment in Martin–Bell syndrome is probably determined by interaction of several genes: simple explanation of phenotypic differences between unaffected and affected males with the same X chromosome. *Human Genetics*, **72**, 248–52.

Sutherland, G. R. (1977). Fragile sites on human chromosomes: Demonstration of their dependence on the type of tissue culture medium. *Science*, **197**, 265–6.

Sutherland, G. R. (1979*a*). Heritable fragile sites on human chromosomes I. Factors affecting expression in lymphocyte culture. *American Journal of Human Genetics*, **31**, 125–35,

Sutherland, G. R. (1979*b*). Heritable fragile sites on human chromosomes II. Distribution, phenotypic effects and cytogenetics. *American Journal of Human Genetics*, **31**, 136–48.

Sutherland, G. R. (1979*c*). Heritable fragile sites on human chromosomes III. Detection of fra(X)(q27) in males with X-linked mental retardation and in their female relatives. *Human Genetics*, **53**, 23–7.

Sutherland, G. R. (1982). Heritable fragile sites on human chromosomes. VIII. Preliminary population cytogenetic data on the folic-acid-sensitive fragile sites. *American Journal of Human Genetics*, **34**, 452–8.

Sutherland, G. R. (1985). Heritable fragile sites on human chromosomes. XII.

Population Cytogenetics. *Annals of Human Genetics*, **49**, 153–61.

Sutherland, G. R. and Hecht, F. (1985). *Fragile sites on human chromosomes.* Oxford Monographs on Medical Genetics, no. 13. Oxford University Press, Oxford.

Sutherland, G. R. and Baker, E. (1986). Effects of nucleotides on expression of the folate sensitive fragile sites. *American Journal of Human Genetics*, **23**, 409–18.

Sutherland, G. R., Baker, E., and Fratini, A. (1985). Excess thymidine induces folate sensitive fragile sites. *American Journal of Medical Genetics*, **22**, 433–43.

Sutherland, G. R., Baker, E., Purvis-Smith, S., Hockey, A., Krumins, E., and Eichenbaum, S. Z. (1987). Prenatal diagnosis of the fragile X using thymidine induction. *Prenatal Diagnosis*, **7**, 197–202.

Tejada, I., Boué, J., and Gilgenkrantz, S. (1983). Diagnostic prénatal sur les cellules du liquide amniotique d'un foetus mâle, porteur du chromosome X fragile. *Annales de Génétique*, **26**, 247–50.

Tommerup, N. (1986). *Induction of the fragile X with simultaneous demonstration of early and late replicating regions and sister chromatid exchanges.* Abstract, 7th International Congress of Human Genetics, Berlin, West Germany, p. 221.

Tommerup, N. (1987*a*). Triradial configurations indicate that expression of the fragile site at Xq27 is non-lethal. *Annales de Génétique*, **30**, 231–2.

Tommerup, N. (1987*b*). *Evidence for a DNA polymerase directed replicative process involved in the expression of the fragile site at Xq27.* Abstract, Third International Workshop on the Fragile X and X-linked Mental Retardation. Troina, 13–16 September.

Tommerup, N. (1987*c*). Analysis of site-specific sister chromatid exchanges at the fragile site at Xq27. Abstract, Third International Workshop on the Fragile X and X-linked Mental Retardation. Troina, 13–16 September.

Tommerup, N. (1988). Induction of the fra(X) in amniotic fluid cells by excess thymidine. *American Journal of Medical Genetics*, **30**, 451–53.

Tommerup, N., Poulsen, H., and Nielsen, K. B. (1981). 5-fluoro-2′-deoxyuridine induction of the fragile site on Xq28 associated with X linked mental retardation. *Journal of Medical Genetics*, **18**, 374–6.

Tommerup, N., Søndergaard, F., Tønnesen, T., Kristensen, M., Arveiler, B., and Schinzel, A. (1985). First trimester prenatal diagnosis of a male fetus with fragile X. *Lancet*, **i**, 870.

Tommerup, N. *et al.* (1986*a*). Second trimester prenatal diagnosis of the fragile X. *American Journal of Medical Genetics*, **23**, 313–24.

Tommerup, N., Holmgren, G., and Steinbach, P. (1986*b*). Fragile X: carrier detection in pregnancy. *American Journal of Medical Genetics*, **23**, 527–30.

Tommerup, N., Tranebjaerg, L., Tønnesen, T., Kastern, W., Hansen, H., and Dissing, J. (1987*a*). Identical expression of the fragile X but discordant clinical affection in two monozygotic twins with Martin–Bell syndrome. Abstract, Third International Workshop on the Fragile X and X-linked Mental Retardation, Troina, 13–16 September.

Tommerup, N. *et al.* (1987*b*). *First trimester prental diagnosis of the fragile size at*

Xq27. Abstract, Third International Workshop on the Fragile X and X-linked Mental Retardation, Troina, 13–16 September.

Tommerup, N., Reintoft, I., Reske-Nielsen, E., Nielsen, K. B., and Mikkelsen, M. (1987*c*). *Unsuspected prenatal diagnosis of the fragile X.* Abstract, Third International Workshop on the Fragile X and X-linked Mental Retardation, Troina, 13–16 September.

Tommerup, N., Laing, S., Christensen, I. J., and Turner, G. (1988). Screening for the fragile X: How many cells should we analyse? *American Journal of Medical Genetics*, **30**, 417–22.

Tuckerman, E., Webb, T., and Bundey, S. E. (1985). Frequency and replication status of the fragile X, fra(X)(q27–28), in a pair of monozygotic twins of markedly differing intelligence. *Journal of Medical Genetics*, **22**, 85–91.

Tuckerman, E., Webb, T., and Thake, A. (1986). Replication status of fragile X(q27.3) in 13 female heterozygotes. *Journal of Medical Genetics*, **23**, 407–10.

Turner, G. and Jacobs, P. A. (1983). Marker (X) linked mental retardation. In *Advances in human genetics*, (ed. M. Harris and K. Hirschhorn), Vol. 13, pp. 83–112. Plenum, New York.

Turner, G. and Partington, M. W. (1988). Fragile X expression, age and the degree of mental handicap in the male. *American Journal of Medical Genetics*, **30**, 423–8.

Turner, G., Brookwell, R., Daniel, A., DeSelikowitz, M., and Zilibowitz, M. (1980). Heterozygous expression of X-linked mental retardation and X-chromosome marker fra(X)(q27). *New England Journal of Medicine*, **303**, 622–44.

Turner, G., Robinson, H., Laing, S., and Purvis-Smith, S. (1986). Preventive screening for the fragile X syndrome. *New England Journal of Medicine*, **315**, 607–9.

Uchida, I. A. and Joyce, E. M. (1982). Activity of the fragile X in heterozygous carriers. *American Journal of Human Genetics*, **34**, 286–93.

Uchida, I. A., Freeman, V. C. P., Jamro, H., Partington, M. W., and Soltan, H. C. (1983). Additional evidence for fragile X activity in heterozygous carriers. *American Journal of Human Genetics*, **35**, 861–8.

Vekemans, M., Popovich, B., Rosenblatt, D., and Monroe, P. (1983). Chromosomal breakage in normal and fragile X subjects using low folate culture conditions. *Journal of Medical Genetics*, **20**, 404–7.

Venter, P. A. *et al.* (1984). A confirmed prenatal diagnosis of a female fetus with the fragile X chromosome. *Prenatal Diagnosis*, **4**, 473–4.

Wang, J. C. and Erbe, R. W. (1985). Thymidylate metabolism in fragile X syndrome cells. *Somatic Cell and Molecular Genetics*, **11**, 353–7.

Wang, J. C., Beardsley, G. P., and Erbe, R. W. (1985). Antifolate-induced misincorporation of deoxyuridine monophosphate into DNA by cells from patients with the fragile X syndrome. *American Journal of Medical Genetics*, **21**, 691–6.

Warren, S. T. (1988). Fragile X syndrome: a hypothesis regarding the molecular mechanism of the phenotype. *American Journal of Medical Genetics*, **30**, 681–8.

Warren, S. T. and Davidson, R. L. (1984). Expression of the fragile X chromosome in human-rodent somatic cell hybrids. *Somatic Cell and Molecular Genetics*, **10**, 409–13.

Warren, S. T., Zhang, F., Licameli, G. R. and Peters, J. F. (1987). The fragile X site in somatic cell hybrids: An approach for molecular cloning of fragile sites. *Science*, in press.

Watson, M. S. *et al.* (1988). Aneuploidy and the fragile X syndrome. *American Journal of Medical Genetics*, **30**, 115–21.

Webb, G. C., Rogers, J. G., Pitt, D. B., Halliday, J., and Theobald, T. (1981). Transmission of fragile (X)(q27) site from a male. *Lancet*, **ii**, 1231–2.

Webb, T., Butler, D., Insley, J., Weaver, J. B., Green, S., and Rodeck, C. (1981). Prenatal diagnosis of Martin–Bell syndrome asociated with fragile site at Xq27–28. *Lancet*, **ii**, 1423.

Webb, T. P., Bundey, S. E., Thake, A. I., and Todd, J. (1986). Population incidence and segregation ratios in the Martin–Bell syndrome. *American Journal of Medical Genetics*, **23**, 573–80.

Webb, T. P., Rodeck, C. H., Nicolaides, K. H., and Gosden, C. M. (1987). Prenatal diagnosis of the fragile X syndrome using fetal blood and amniotic fluid. *Prenatal Diagnosis*, **7**, 203–14.

Wenger, S. L., Hennesey, J. C. and Steele, M. W. (1987). Increased sister chromatid exchange freuquency at Xq27 site in affected fragile X males. *American Journal of Medical Genetics*, **26**, 909–14.

Wilhelm, D., Froster-Iskenius, U., Paul, J., and Schwinger, E. (1988). Fra(X) frequency on the active X-chromosome and phenotype in heterozygous carriers of the fra(X) form of mental retardation. *American Journal of Medical Genetics*, **30**, 407–15.

Wilmot, P. L., Shapiro, L. R., and Duncan, P. A. (1980). The Xq27 fragile site and 47,XXY. *American Journal of Human Genetics*, **32**, 94A.

Wilson, M. G. and Marchese, C. A. (1984). Prenatal diagnosis of fragile X in a heterozygous female fetus and postnatal follow-up. *Prenatal Diagnosis*, **4**, 61–6.

Yunis, J. J. and Soreng, A. L. (1984). Constitutive fragile sites and cancer. *Science*, **226**, 1199–204.

Zeeland, A. A. van *et al.* (1982). Effects of aphidicolin on repair replication and induced chromosomal aberrations in mammalian cells. *Mutation Research* **92**, 379–92.

Index